LIFE AND TEACHING *of the* MASTERS OF THE FAR EAST

VOLUME II

By Baird T. Spalding

DeVorss Publications
Marina del Rey, California

Volume 2
ISBN: 0-87516-364-5

6 Volume set
ISBN: 0-87516-538-9

DeVorss & Company, Publisher
P.O. Box 550
Marina del Rey, CA 90294

Printed in The United States of America

THE LIFE AND TEACHING
OF THE
MASTERS OF THE FAR EAST

By BAIRD T. SPALDING

Baird T. Spalding, whose name became legend in metaphysical and truth circles during the first half of the 20th century, played an important part in introducing to the Western world the knowledge that there are Masters, or Elder Brothers, who are assisting and guiding the destiny of mankind. The countless numbers of letters that have come in through the years, from all over the world, bear testimony of the tremendous help received from the message in these books.

Partial listing of the contents of the six volumes:

Volume 1: Introduction of the Master Emil — Visit to the "Temple of Silence" — Astral projection — Walking on Water — Visit to the Healing Temple — Emil talks about America — The Snowmen of the Himalayas — New Light on the teachings of Jesus.

Volume II: Visit to the Temple of the Great Tau Cross — Visit with the Master Jesus — Jesus discusses the nature of hell; the nature of God — The Mystery of thought vibrations — Jesus feeds the multitude — An account of a healing experience — Jesus and Buddha visit the group.

Volume III: One of the masters speaks of the Christ consciousness — The nature of cosmic energy — The creation of the planets and the worlds — The trip to Lhasa — Visit at the Temple Pora-tat-sanga — Explaining the mystery of levitation — A doubter becomes convinced of the existence of Jesus.

Volume IV: This material was first presented as "The India Tour Lessons." Each chapter has text for study, as well as guides to teachers for developing and interpreting the material. Among subjects covered: The White Brotherhood — The One Mind — Basis of coming social reorganization — Prana.

Volume V: Material taken from lectures given by Mr. Spalding in California during the last two years of his life. There is also a brief biographical sketch. Partial contents: Camera of past events — Is there a God — The divine pattern — The reality — Mastery over death — The law of supply.

Volume VI: 18 articles by Mr. Spalding, with questions & answers, taken from *Mind Magazine*, 1935-1937, and a contemporary biographical sketch of Spalding. A special section includes rare photos of Spalding, the India Tour group, shipboard accommodations, Calcutta; also letters from the tour and other Spalding memorabilia. Seven manuscripts by Spalding include: Original of the Lord's Prayer — Divine Mastery — Eternal Youth — Rising Out of Limitation — The Power of Thought. A eulogy and reminiscences by friends of Spalding are included.

❦

FOREWORD

I N publishing this, the Second Volume of *Life and Teaching of the Masters of the Far East*, I am purposely omitting names of people and places. I feel that I am at liberty to withhold names of places and locations, according the reader the privilege of accepting as fact or fiction, as he deems expedient, the accounts set forth herein, remarking only that facts are at times more astonishing than fiction.

At the time of taking up this work it was definitely understood that nothing should be published officially until the work had progressed to the degree where deductions could be reached regarding the life and teaching of these people.

With the above statements fixed firmly in mind, I am presenting for the reader's consideration the *Life and Teaching of the Masters of the Far East*, Vol. II.

In this I sincerely and with all respect remind the reader that the more receptive one is, the more one receives.

(Signed) BAIRD T. SPALDING

CHAPTER I

THE morning of January 1st found us up early with faculties alert. Everyone seemed to feel that there was something ahead that would make our past experiences but stepping-stones for those to come.

As we gathered around the breakfast table the friend joined us whom we had met on the roof of Emil's home in the little village where we had stopped while on our way here. You will recall him as the one who interpreted my dream. After exchanging greetings, he said, "You have been with us for more than a year. You have traveled with us and lived among us and shared our lives and you no doubt have confidence in us. As you will be with us until April or May, I have come to invite you to go to the temple of the Great Tau Cross, which you have observed is cut in the rock of the cliff just outside the village."

We found afterwards that the rooms of this temple were cut from the rock that formed a perpendicular cliff over six hundred feet high. The openings that formed the rooms were cut deep enough into the walls so that all walls were of rock. Wherever it was necessary to place windows to admit light and air, openings had been cut through the outer wall of the cliff, which faced south. The openings for the windows were about eight feet square and each room had two openings, except the first or lower room. This room had only one opening, which communicated with a large crevasse that was worn in the rock wall just east of the temple. When the rooms of the temple were cut from the rock, this room had no opening other than the entrance which was from a tunnel cut from the solid rock and terminating in the crevasse mentioned. The opening for the window was put in later. Originally the entrance to the tunnel was hidden under a great boulder which was one of a mass that had fallen from the sides of the cliff and lodged on a projecting shelf; and this boulder had been so arranged that it could be dropped into place from the passageway. When in place, it could not be moved from the outside. The only way of reaching this shelf was by a ladder about fifty feet long that could be raised or lowered from above. The openings that served as windows were fitted with great flat stones that fitted into grooves at the bottom, so that they could be slid into place. When they were in place there was, to one standing in the village, no appearance of an opening. We were told that this construction was resorted to for protection from the marauding bands that infested the country farther north. These bands at times came as far south as this village. The village had been destroyed a number of times but the people had not been harmed, as they could take refuge in the temple. This temple had not been built by our friends but had been acquired by them from the villagers, to be used as a place to keep numerous records which they prized very highly. After their acquisition of the temple the raids ceased, the village had not been molested, and they all lived in peace.

It is claimed that some of these records date back to the period of man's advent upon this earth; that these records are those of the Naacals, or Holy Brothers, as they were called, and that they came direct from the Motherland of Man. It is also claimed that these Holy Brothers came direct to Burma and taught the Nagas. These records seem to prove that

8

the forefathers of these people were the authors of
the Sourya Siddhanta and the Earlier Vedas. The
Sourya Siddhanta is the oldest known work on astro-
nomy. These records place it back 25,000 years; the
Earlier Vedas they place back 45,000 years. It is not
claimed that these are all originals and were brought
here to be preserved. It is claimed that these were
copied from the same records that the Babylonian
records were taken from. It is also claimed that the
originals from which these were copied are the original Osirian and Atlantean records.

The rooms of this temple were arranged one above
the other for seven stories and communication between the rooms was by means of a series of stone
steps cut in the solid rock. The opening to gain
access to the stairway was at one corner of the room
and communicated directly with the stairway, which
rose at an angle of forty-five degrees until it reached
a landing about eight feet square where the entrance
to the room above was cut. There was about eight
feet of solid rock left between the ceiling of the room
below and the floor of the room above. The ceiling
of the upper room of the seventh story terminated
about twelve feet below a wide jutting ledge of rocks
about one hundred feet from the top of the preci-
pice. A stairway led from this room up through an
opening that communicated with the center room,
so that a diagram of the whole structure would represent a huge Tau Cross.

The rooms above were cut so that the ledge formed a porch or balcony and the entrances were from
the ledge. The cliff was soft, coarse-grained granite.
The work evidently had been done with crude hand
implements and it must have taken years to accomplish. It is claimed that not a piece of timber was
used when the temple was constructed. After it was
acquired by our friends, they put in timber and the

rooms were all very comfortable, especially on sunshiny days.

We learned that since they had acquired the temple the windows had hever been closed nor the entrance barred, yet very few had ever visited there unless they had seen and knew something of the true spiritual enlightenment.

Our friend continued, "This day is to you the beginning of a new year, the old having passed out as it were, from your life, never to return, except possibly in thought, as the memory of its pleasures, its sorrows and cares, and the more engrossing thoughts of business come flooding back. Aside from that, it is forgotten, gone; to you a page torn from the year-book of your life. We look upon it as a period of attainment and added triumph, an ongoing, a span carrying us on to a more glorious development and achievement; a time of greater promise and enlightenment; a time when we can be of greater service; when we can be younger, stronger, and more loving from each succeeding experience. Your thought is, 'Why?' Our answer is, 'to draw your own conclusion, choose your own life.'

Our Chief said, without any thought of intruding, "We wish to see and know."

Our friend resumed, "From this time on, there are definite lessons for those who do not see and know or grasp the full meaning of the goal of life well lived. This does not mean a life of asceticism and austerity, and aloofness or sadness. This means a life of accomplishment in joy and gladness, where all sorrows, all pain, are banished forever."

Then, in a lighter and more whimsical mood he said, "You have expressed a desire to see and know. The desire is no sooner expressed than it is fulfilled. The thought expressed in a verse in your Bible comes to me as I look over this assembly, 'Where two or

10

three are gathered together in My Name, there will I
be also.' How often that verse has been looked upon
as a mere play upon words, instead of being applied
and made really true. The great error you have
made with Jesus' teachings is, you have consigned
them to the dim and misty past, looking upon them
as mythical and mystical, pointing to something that
may be gained after death, instead of knowing that
they can be applied in the daily lives of all, right here
and now, if you only will.

"We wish it to be understood that we are not
putting forth the claim that Jesus, as the Christ,
represented a plane or condition of life in his own
realization that had not been brought forth to a
greater or lesser degree by a great many seers and
prophets of other times and peoples. We wish to
emphasize his life because that life is the one you can
understand more fully. The specific reference to his
own life can have but one purpose and meaning and
that was the faith-inspiring fact that his life and
experience was the living demonstration of his teachings. The speculative dogma of vicarious atonement,
which has biased Christian thought for centuries,
can not be charged to the author of the Sermon on
the Mount or the Parable of the Prodigal Son.

"The leaders of Christian thought have diverted
the followers of Jesus and his teachings from their
practical application and the study of the God power.
They have taught them to look upon his teachings as
the experiences of the Apostles after his time, instead
of teaching them that the law upon which those
teachings were based was an exact science which
could be understood and experienced in the lives of
all.

"The Orientals have made the scientific phase of
their religion the supreme object of their study and
attainment. In this they have gone to the other ex-

treme. In this way both have consigned their religion to the realm of the miraculous and supernatural. The one has become absorbed in the wholly ethical, while the other has become absorbed in the scientific side only. Thus both have shut out true spirituality.

"The monastic life of retirement, asceticism, and seclusion from the world, whether in Buddhistic or Christian monasteries, is neither a necessity nor is it the true method of attaining spiritual enlightenment nor the realization of the perfect life of wisdom and power as brought forth by Jesus.

"These monastic systems have been in existence for many thousands of years, yet they have in no wise accomplished as much for the uplift of the common people as did the teachings of Jesus in the few short years of his time here on earth.

"It is very well known that he embraced all their teachings, going through the initiations and studying the so-called sacred mysteries, the ritualistic forms and ceremonies, until he came to the teachings of Osiris. These were interpreted to him by a priest who had held himself aloof from all the ritualistic, monastic, and materialistic forms of worship.

"This priest was a follower of King Thoth, of the First Dynasty of the Egyptian Kings. When King Thoth declared Egypt an empire, he did it under the power of a dictator and usurper of the people's rights. Centuries before these people had built up and maintained a glorious civilization of unity and brotherhood under the guidance and direction of Osiris and his followers. These people were the pure white race and were always known as the Israelites, of whome the Hebrew race is a division. Thoth ruled wisely and attempted to maintain the Osirian teachings but, after his day, the dark and material concept crept in, as the Egyptian or dark hordes from the south, who had swept him into power, gained

12

sway. The succeeding dynasties fell away from Osirian teachings, gradually took up the dark concept of the dark race, and finally practiced black magic entirely. Their kingdom soon fell, as all such kingdoms must fall.

"After Jesus had listened attentively to this priest and his teachings, he recognized their deep, inner meaning. He also saw, through the insight which he had received from Buddhistic teachings, that there was a great similarity underlying the two. He then determined to go to India, over the old caravan route maintained at that time.

"There he studied the Buddhistic teachings which had been preserved with a reasonable degree of purity. He saw that, in spite of the ritualistic forms and dogmas that had been imposed by man, religion had but one source and that was the God within, Whom he designated as his Father and the Father of all. Then he threw all forms to the winds, as it were, and went directly to God, went straight to the heart of this loving attainment. He soon found that this did not take long years of weary plodding through dogmas, rituals, creeds, formulas, and initiations which the priesthood were foisting upon the people in order to hold them in ignorance and, therefore, in subjection. He realized that that for which he was seeking was right within himself. He knew that in order to be the Christ he must declare that he was the Christ. Then with pure motive of life, thought, word, and deed he must live the life he sought, in order to incorporate it within his physical body. Then, after perceiving this, he had the courage to go out and declare it to all the world.

"It did not matter from whom or where he got his realization. It was the work that counted, not what someone else had done but what he did, that counted. The common people, whose cause he sponsored,

13

heard him gladly. He did not borrow his precepts from India, Persia, or Egypt. Their teachings were but the outer that brought him to see his own God-head and the Christ, the representation of it, that was in every one; not in a few but in all.

"Osiris was born in Atlantis more than thirty-five thousand years ago. The chroniclers of his life, long after his time, called him a god because of his wonderful works. He was direct descendant of those of higher thought who had kept their concepts clear in the Motherland of Man.

"It was so of the great portion of all the mythological characters that have been brought down to us. Their works and characters have been distorted by repetition and translation of the stories concerning them. Their works and attainments were looked upon as supernatural by those who would not give the time and thought to go into the deeper meaning and find that they were divinely natural to man in his true dominion.

"The chroniclers deified Osiris, then they began making images of him. These images only represented what he stood for, at first. Then, gradually the images became fixed in the mind, the ideal was forgotten, and the empty idol remained.

"Buddha was another who was deified by the chroniclers long after his time. Note the images of him that have been set up, with the result that the image is worshipped instead of the ideal. Again the empty idol. It is the same with signs and symbols.

"The teachings that Buddha received came from the same source as did those of Osiris but in a different way. The teachings that Buddha contacted came from the Motherland direct to Burma, brought there by the Naacals. Osiris' teachings came direct to him, as his forefathers lived in the Motherland, and when he was a young man he had gone to the Motherland to study. After finishing his studies he returned home, became the leader of the Atlanteans and brought the people back to the worship of the God within, as they were gradually slipping back to the dark concept, influenced by the dark races about them.

"Moses was another leader whose followers and chroniclers deified him after his time. He was an Israelite and contacted the records of the Babylonians, receiving his teachings from them. These records form a part of our Bible. What Moses saw and learned from these records was written by him in the exact form and words. The facts which he put down were badly distorted by translators. I could go on and recall many more.

"Jesus saw and contacted all their teachings, then, in his characteristic manner, went to the heart of all these. He went one step further than any of them did, by glorifying his body to the point where he could allow it to be crucified; yet he brought it forth in a triumphant resurrection.

"Studying the teachings of Osiris, Buddha, and Jesus, you will find many similarities; in fact, at times you will find the same words used. Yet did any of them copy? The teachings showed them the way from the outer to the inner. Then they must have dropped all teaching, all copying, and must have gone beyond it all. Had any of them just copied and studied what they saw and were taught and then had not been able to see that all was from the God right within themselves, they would have been studying yet and their lives and experiences would never have been recorded.

"They all went through the same experience in that their followers wanted to crown them kings of temporal kingdoms; but to this they would not listen, each expressing the same thought in almost the same words, 'My kingdom is not of the material, it is spiritual.' With Osiris it went so far that the later chroniclers placed him as an Egyptian king."

Here the talk ended and we all walked to the temple. As we arrived in the lower room, our friend began, "In ascending from room to room of this temple, please remember that no man can confer any rights upon another. By developing your under-standing you will find that you are the equal of any man and he who attempts to confer his rights or what he has upon you is not consistent, as he is attempting to give what he can not. One may point the way to his brother, that he may extend his vision to incorporate the good, but he cannot confer that good which he himself has, upon him."

By this time we had arrived in the second room, where four of our friends from the village had prece-ded us. After a few moments of general talk, all were seated and our teacher resumed. "There is not a character in all your history that stands out as Jesus does. You count your time before and after his birth. He is idolized by a majority of your people and that is where they err. Instead of the idol, he should be the ideal; instead of being made into a graven im-age, he should be real and living to you, for he actually lives today in the same body in which he was crucified. He lives and can talk to you just as he could before that event. The great error with so many is that they see his life ending in sorrow and death upon the cross, forgetting entirely that the greater portion of his life is that portion after the resurrection. He is able to teach and heal, today, far more than he ever did before. You can come into His presence at any time, if you will. If you seek, you will find him. He is not a king who can intrude his presence upon you but a mighty brother who stands ready always to help you and to help the world.

When he lived upon the mortal, earthly plane, he was able to reach but a few. Today he is able to reach all who will look to him.

"Did he not say: 'Where I am, there you are also'? Does that mean that he is away in a place called heaven that you must die to attain? He is where you are and he is able to walk and talk with you. Lift your sight a little higher and let it extend to a wider horizon; and if your heart and thought are sincerely with him, you will see him. You may walk and talk with him. If you look closely you will find the scars of the cross, the spear and the thorns, all healed, all gone, and the radiant love and happiness about him will tell you that they are all forgotten, forgiven."

Our friend stopped talking and all was deep silence for the space of about five minutes. Then the room lighted up with a brilliance that we had not seen before. We heard a voice. At first it seemed a long way off and indistinct. After our attention was attracted to it and our thoughts directed to it, the voice became very distinct and rang out in clear bell-like tones.

One of our party asked, "Who is speaking?" Our Chief said, "Please be silent. Our dear Master, Jesus, is speaking." Then one of our friends said, "You are right, Jesus speaks."

Then the voice went on, "When I said 'I am the way, the truth and the life,' I did not intend to convey the thought to mankind that I, Myself, was the only true light. 'As many as are led by the Spirit of God, they are sons of God.' When I said, 'I am the perfect Son, the only begotten Son of God in whom the Father is well pleased,' I fully intended to convey the thought to all mankind that one of God's children saw, understood, and claimed his divinity; saw that he lived, moved, and had his being in God, the great Father-Mother Principle of all things; that

17

seeing this, he then spoke forth the word that he was the Christ, the only begotten Son of God, and with true heart and steadfast purpose lived the life, becoming what he claimed to be. With his eyes fixed upon that ideal, he filled his whole body with that ideal, and the end sought was fulfilled.

"The reason so many have not seen me is that they have put me upon a shrine and placed me in the unapproachable. They have surrounded me with miracles and mystery; and again, they have placed me far from the common people, whom I love dearly. I love them with a love that is unspeakable. I have not withdrawn from them. They have withdrawn from me. They have set up veils, walls and partitions, mediators, and images of myself and those so near and dear to me. They have surrounded us with myth and mystery until we seem so far removed from these dear ones that they do not know how to approach. They pray and supplicate my dear mother and those that surround me, and thus they hold us all in mortal thought. When truly, if they would know us as we are, they would and could shake our hands. If they would drop all superstition and creed and know us as we are, they could talk with us as you do. We are no different at any time than as you see us. How we would love to have the whole world know this. Then what an awakening, what a reunion, what a feast!

"You have surrounded us so long in mystery, it is no wonder that doubt and disbelief have become dominant. The more you build images and idols and surround us with death and make us unapproachable, save through some other than ourselves, the deeper the doubt and shadow will be cast and the chasm of superstition grow wider and more difficult to cross. If you would boldly shake our hands and say, 'I know you,' then all could see and know us as

18

we are. There is no mystery surrounding us or those we love, for we love the whole world.

"So many see only that part of my life which ended on the cross, forgetting that the greater part is as I am now; forgetting entirely that man still lives, even after what seems a violent death. Life cannot be destroyed. It goes on and on and life well lived never degenerates nor passes. Even the flesh may be immortalized so that it never changes.

"Dear Pilate, when he washed his hands and said, 'Away with him and crucify him yourselves, I find no fault in him,' how little he knew of the history he was making or of the prophecy he was fulfilling. He, with the multitude, has suffered far more than I have suffered. That is all passed and forgotten, forgiven as you will see by our all standing here in one place together."

Two figures came forth and were embraced by Jesus. As they stood with his hand on the shoulder of one, he said, "This dear brother has come all the way with me. While this one," pointing to the second one, "saw many more trails before his eyes were opened. But after they were fully opened, he came quickly. He is just as true and we love him with the same love we do all others."

Then another advanced slowly and stood for a moment. Jesus turned and with outstretched arms said, "Dear Pilate." There was no mistaking the comradeship of the embrace.

Then Pilate spoke and said, "I labored and suffered many weary years after the verdict which I pronounced that day so lightly when I cast from myself the burden. How few of us while in the material realize the needless burdens we heap upon others in the attempt to shift the responsibility from ourselves. It is only when our eyes are opened that we realize the more we attempt to shirk and shift our

19

burdens upon others, the greater the burden bears down upon us. It took many weary years before my eyes were opened to this fact; but since the day they were opened, how I have rejoiced."

Then the invisible choir burst into full song and the melody beggars all description. After a few bars, Jesus stepped forward and said, "Do you wonder that I have long ago forgiven those that nailed me to the cross? Then why have not all forgiven, as I have? With me the forgiveness was complete when I said, 'It is finished.' Why do you not see me as I am, not nailed to the cross, but risen above all mortality?"

Again the invisible choir continued with "Hail, all hail, you Sons of God. Hail, hail and praise Him. His kingdom endures forever among men. Lo, God is with you always"; and as they sang, the words stood out in raised letters upon the wall of the room.

This was not a far-off, hazy, nearly invisible scene. Neither was it set on a stage far away from us. All were actually present in the room, for we talked with them, shook hands with them, and photographed them. The only difference that we could see between them and ourselves was the peculiar light about them and this appeared to be the source of the light in the room. There were no shadows anywhere. To us there seemed to be a peculiar translucent quality about the flesh, for when we touched them or clasped their hands, the flesh seemed like alabaster. Still, it had a warm, friendly glow and that same warmth pervaded everything about them. Even after they had walked out, the room we were in retained the same warmth and light. Every time we entered the room afterward, some of the party would remark about it.

One day, a short time after, our party had gathered in the room, and we were talking of how the room impressed us, when our Chief said to me, "It is sublime." He had expressed the feelings of everyone and there was no more said about it. When we returned that fall, the room seemed a sanctuary and we spent many hours there.

Our party waited while the others filed from the room. As Pilate started to leave, he motioned our Chief to join him and together all descended the stairs, down to the lower room through the passage-way to the crevasse and down the ladders, one by one, until all had descended. Then all dispersed in the usual manner, as if the meeting were a common occurrence.

After the guests had departed, we gathered a-round our hostess and each in turn clasped her hand to thank her for the remarkable evening we had experienced. One of our party said, "The only way I can express my thoughts and feelings is to say that my narrow, mortal outlook has been completely shattered." He apparently struck the key that vibrat-ed to all our thoughts. I did not attempt to give voice to my thoughts or feelings; neither have I ever attempted to record them. I shall leave that for the reader to imagine. After leaving our hostess to retire, there was not a word spoken. Each one seemed to feel that an entire new world had opened.

CHAPTER II

THE next morning, after we had gathered for breakfast, we questioned our hostess and found it was not an uncommon occurrence for Jesus to come as he did; and she said he often came and joined the others in their healing work.

After breakfast we found that our hostess and two other ladies were to accompany us to the temple that day. As we left the house, two men joined the party. One told our hostess that there was a sick child in the village who was asking for her. We followed the men to the home of the child and found it very ill. Our hostess walked forward and held out her hands. The mother placed the child in her arms. Instantly the little one's face brightened. Then it snuggled up close for a moment and in a few minutes was sound asleep. Our hostess returned the child to the mother and we proceeded to the temple. On the way she remarked, "Oh, if these dear people would only see and do this work for themselves, instead of depending upon us. It would be so much better for them. As it is, they let us entirely alone until some emergency arises, then they call for us, which is quite all right, except that it does not give them any self-reliance whatever. We would much prefer to see them self-reliant but they are child-like in every way."

By this time we had reached the foot of the ladder. We went up and entered the tunnel. The two men accompanied us. As this tunnel was through solid rock, it was natural to suppose that it would be dark. But it was lighted sufficiently to enable us to see objects for a considerable distance ahead; and the light seemed to be around us so that there were no shadows. We had noticed this the day before but no one had remarked about it. Upon making inquiry, we were told that the light was around us just as it appeared to be and that when there was no one in the tunnel it was dark.

We went on through the tunnel and up the stairs to the third room. This room was somewhat larger than the two below and there were a great many tablets stored along two walls. Just back of this room we found that another large room had been excavated and later learned that this room was also filled with similar tablets. These tablets were of a reddish dark-brown color, quite well glazed. Some were about 14 x 24 inches and about two inches thick and weighed from ten to twelve pounds each. Others were much larger. We were puzzled to know how these could have been transported over the mountains. We expressed our wonderment at this time and were told that they were not transported over the mountains but were brought to the Gobi country when it was fertile and well settled, before mountains were raised. Then long after the mountains came up, the tablets were removed to this place to guard against any possibility of their being destroyed.

It is claimed that before the mountains rose, a great tidal wave ran over a portion of the country, totally devastating it and a large part of the population. Those who survived were cut off from the world and a means of livelihood and they became the forefathers of the roving bands of brigands which infest the Gobi at this time. It is claimed that the Great Uigur Empire existed where the Himalayas and the Gobi are today; that large cities of a people in a high state of civilization existed there and that drifting sand covered the ruins after they were destroyed by the water. We afterwards took the descriptions as they were translated to us from the tablets and found three of these cities; and we believe that some day, when further excavations are completed, they will prove the authenticity of these records and that which is claimed for them. These records place the date of this civilization back hundreds of thousands of years. As this is not a treatise on research, I feel that I have digressed.

We were shown through the different rooms. During the general conversation it developed that one of the men who joined our party in the morning was a descendant of the man whom we met in the village where John the Baptist had lived and whom we called our friend of the records. This man showed every sign of advanced years, which caused us to wonder.

While we were returning to the first room, our Chief asked if a desire could be fulfilled as soon as it was expressed. Our hostess answered that if the desire were put forth in true form it would be fulfilled. She then went on to say that desire is but a form of prayer, that it was the true form of prayer which Jesus used, as his prayers were answered; that prayer which is always answered must be true prayer, therefore must be scientific and, if scientific, must be according to fixed law.

Continuing, she said, "The law is 'As you know, your prayer is granted,' and 'What things you desire, when you pray, know you receive them and you shall have them.' If we know positively that whatever we have asked for is ours already, we may know that we are working in accordance with the law. If the desire is filled, then we may know that the law is fulfilled. If the desire is not filled, then we must know that we have asked amiss. We should know that the fault is with us and not with God.

"Then the instructions are, 'You shall love the Lord, your God, with all your heart, with all your soul, with all your mind, and with all your strength.' Now go deep, deep down within your own soul — not with forebodings, fear, and unbelief, but with a glad, free, thankful heart, knowing that that which you stand in need of is already yours.

"The secret lies in getting the at-one-ment; getting the consciousness of it and then holding firmly and never deviating, though all earth should oppose. 'Of myself I can do nothing,' said Jesus, 'The Father that dwells in me, He does the work.' Have faith in God. Have faith and doubt not. Have faith and fear not. Now remember there is no limitation to God's power. 'All things are possible.'

"Use positive words in making your request. There is naught but the perfect condition desired. Then plant in your soul the perfect seed idea and that alone. Now ask to manifest health and not to be healed of disease; to express harmony and realize abundance — not to be delivered from inharmony, misery and limitations. Throw these off as you would discard an old garment. They are old and only outgrown things; you can afford to discard them joyfully. Do not even turn to gaze upon them. They are no-thing — nothing.

"Fill the seemingly blank spaces about you with the thought of God, Infinite Good. Then remember the word God is a seed. It must grow.

"Leave the how, when, and where to God. Your work is merely to say what you want and to give forth blessings, knowing that the moment you have asked, you have received. All the details of this bringing forth is the work of the Father. Remember, He does

25

the work. Do faithfully your part; leave and trust God's part to Him. Ask. Affirm. Look to God for what you want; then receive God's fulfillment.

"Keep the thought of God's abundance always in mind. If any other thought comes, replace it with that of God's abundance and bless that abundance. Give thanks constantly, if need be, that the work is done. Do not go back again to the asking. Just bless and give thanks that the work is done, that God is working in you, that you are receiving that which you desire, for you desire only the good that you may give out the good to all. Let this be in silence and in secret. Pray to your Father in secret, and your Father who sees the secret of your soul will reward you openly.

"When the demonstration is complete, you will look back upon the time faithfully given as one of your greatest treasures. You will have proved the law and you will realize the power of your word spoken in faith and blessing. Remember that God has perfected His plan. He has poured out and is continuously pouring out, lovingly and lavishly upon us, all good and every good thing that we can desire. Again He says, 'Try Me and see if I will not open the windows of heaven and pour out such a blessing there will not be room to receive it.'

With All My Heart

"In the heart of my being, Father, I am one with You, and I recognize You as Being, the Father of all. You are Spirit, Omnipresent, Omnipotent, Omniscient. You are Wisdom, Love, and Truth; the power and substance and intelligence of which and through which all things are created. You are the life of my spirit, the substance of my soul, the intelligence of my thought. I am expressing You in my body and in my affairs. You are the beginning and

26

the end, the very All of the good which I can express. The desire of my thought which is implanted in my soul is quickened by your life in my spirit; and in the fullness of time, through the law of faith, it is brought into visibility in my experience. I know that the good I desire already exists in Spirit in invisible form and but awaits the fulfillment of the law to be made visible and I know that already I have.

With All My Soul

"The words which I now speak outline to You, my Father, that which I desire. As a seed it is planted in the soil of my soul and moved upon by Your quickening life in my spirit. It must come forth. I allow only Your Spirit—Wisdom, Love and Truth—to move in my soul. I desire only that which is good for all and I now ask You, Father, to bring it forth.

"Father, within me I ask to express Love, Wisdom, Strength, and Eternal Youth. I ask to realize Harmony, Happiness, and Abundant Prosperity; that I may have the understanding direct from You, of the method of bringing forth from the Universal Substance that which will satisfy every good desire. This is not for self, Father, but that I may have the understanding so that I may be of service to all Your Children.

With All My Mind

"That which I desire is already in visible form. I form in mind only that which I desire. As a seed begins its growth underground in the quiet and in the dark, so does my desire now take form in the silent, invisible realm of my soul. I enter my closet and shut the door. Quietly and confidently I now hold my desire in mind as already fulfilled. Father, I now await the perfect outpictureing of my desire. Father, Father, within me I thank You that now in

27

the invisible the fulfillment of my desire is always established and I know that You have poured out lovingly and lavishly to all an abundance of Your treasure; that You have filled every good desire of my life; that I may partake of Your opulent supply; that I may realize my oneness with You; that all Your children may realize the same; and that whatever I have, I may pour out to help all Your children. All that I have I give to You, Father.

With All My Strength

"No act or thought of mine shall deny that I have already received in Spirit the fulfillment of my desire and it is now brought forth into perfect visibility. In spirit, in soul, in mind, in body, I am true to my desire. I have perceived my good in Spirit. I have conceived it as a perfect idea in soul and I have given true thought form to my desire. I now bring into visibility, or true manifestation, my perfect desire.

"I thank You, Father, that I now have Love, Wisdom, and Understanding; Life, Health, Strength and Eternal Youth; Harmony, Happiness and Abundant Prosperity; and the method of bringing forth from the Universal Substance that which will satisfy every good desire.

" 'Said I not unto you that, if you would believe, you should see the glory of God?' "

After our hostess had spoken, there was deep silence for a moment; then she continued: "Understand that, if it is not finished and your desire is not now visible, the fault is within yourselves and not with God. Do not go back again to the asking but like Elijah, persist, hold out the cup until it is filled; pour out blessings and thanks that it is done now, though every mortal thought of error beset you. *Go on, go on, it is here now, and believe me your faith is rewarded; your faith becomes knowing.*

"We will suppose it is ice you desire. Would you begin by speaking out the word, 'ice,' all about you indiscriminately? If you did, you would scatter your forces in all directions and nothing would come to you. You should first form a mental picture of what you desire, hold it directly in thought just long enough to get the image, then drop the image entirely and look directly into the Universal God Substance. Know that that Substance is a part of God and, therefore, a part of you and in that Substance there is everything you need; that God is pressing that Substance out to you just as fast as you can use it; and that you can never deplete the supply. Then know that everyone who has created that supply has brought forth from this Substance, whether they have done it consciously or unconsciously. Now with your thought and vision fixed on the one central atom, God, hold that atom until you have imprinted your desire upon it. You will lower the vibration of that atom until it becomes ice. Then all the atoms surrounding that one will hasten to obey your desire. Their vibration will be lowered until they will adhere to the central particle and in a moment you will have ice. You do not even need any water about you. You need only the ideal."

Again there was deep silence. In a moment a picture appeared upon the wall of the room. At first the forms were still and we thought but little of it. But then the forms began to move about and we could see their lips move as though they were talking. Immediately our attention became fixed and our hostess said, "This picture is depicting a scene that happened long ago, when the Uigur Empire was at its height. You can see how beautiful the people are and the country is warm and sunny. You can see how the trees are swayed by the breezes. Even the colors are reproduced. There were no fierce storms

29

to disturb the land or its inhabitants. If you will give close attention you will hear them speak and, if you can understand the language, you can tell what they are talking about. You can even see the play of the muscles of the body as they move about."

Our hostess ceased speaking but the pictures continued to pour in, with scenes changing at intervals of about two minutes until we seemed to be a part of the picture, so close did they appear to us. Suddenly there came a scene with three of our party in it. There was no mistaking them. We could hear their voices and recognized what they were talking about. It proved to be an incident that had taken place in South America about ten years previous.

Then our hostess resumed, "We are able to throw thought vibrations into the atmosphere which connect with the thought vibrations of those that have passed and our vibrations collect those of the thoughts gone before until they draw them together at a given point. Then you are able to see those scenes reproduced just as they were when the scenes occurred. This may seem phenomenal to you but it will not be long before your people will be producing pictures similar to these you have seen. The only difference is that they will be photographic and mechanical, while ours are neither.

"The leaders of Christian thought have been so busy with their interdenominational bickerings, each one determined that the other should not succeed, that they have nearly forgotten what true spiritual life means. Likewise, the Oriental people have set themselves so determinedly upon the esoteric, occult and scientific side of their philosophy that they have also passed over the spiritual.

"It will come to a point where a few of those who develop the pictures, through mechanical means, to their higher degree of perfection will be the first to see the true spiritual meaning, the educational value, the benefit to be derived, and the accomplishments that are possible. Then those few will have the courage to step forth and proclaim the accomplishment by the pictures they produce. It will be seen that these devices and the people that develop them — now thought to be the most material — will be the greatest power of any factor brought forth and developed by your people in bringing out the true spiritual idea. Thus, it will be left to those who seem to be the most material of the greatest material race to bring forth the truly spiritual. Your people are going on and will bring forth a device which will reproduce the voices of those who have passed, more accurately than they now reproduce the voices of the living. You are going on and will achieve, in a measure, mechanically, what we do with thought force. This is where you are going to excel all the world in future development.

"The founding of America portrays the white race's homecoming, as that land is their former home and one of the places where the great early spiritual enlightenment was brought forth. Thus it is the land where the greatest spiritual awakening will take place. In a short time you will be far ahead of the whole world in physical and mechanical development. You will go on and develop the physical and mechanical until it is perfected to such a degree that you will see there is but one more step to the spiritual. When that time comes, you will have the courage to take the step. There is a saying in your country that necessity is the mother of invention. Necessity placed you in a position where you were obliged to do that which seemed impossible. Your mode of accomplishment has made you a very material nation. With your mode of living, this has been necessary in order to survive. When you, as a nation, do

31

touch the spiritual realm, the strides that you have made in the material will seem like child's play. With the strong physical bodies and quick perception you have developed, your race will become a light to all other nations; and you will look back and wonder, as you are now looking back and wondering, why your forefathers used the stage-coach and the tallow candle when steam and electricity were all around them, just as it is around you today. Had they abided by the law, they would have received and benefited as you have and will.

"You will find that the spiritual surrounds and is above the material. You will find that in the spiritual there is a higher law and, when you abide by that law, you receive the benefit; for the spiritual is just above and around the mechanical or material. You will find there is no more mystery in the spiritual than there is in the mechanical or the material. The things that appear difficult to you now will be simple, and you will surmount them just as readily as you are now surmounting the mechanical and material. It is the continual striving that does the work."

By this time the old gentleman whom I spoke of before had selected and brought out a tablet and placed it on a nearby easel.

Our hostess went on to say, "The great error which many people make is that they do not look upon lessons as a means of attaining a given end. They do not realize that, when that end is attained and fully recognized, the lessons are to be discarded and the attainment is to be followed. Then, if they still wish to go on, they may pause for a moment and place what they have accomplished in their storehouse (sometimes called the subconscious); and after this step, the lessons leading to the further attainment which they seek may be taken up. But as soon as the goal is reached they must again discard the lessons. In this way they may go on, step by step, to the highest attainment. You will find that lessons are but steps in the stairway; and if you were to attempt to carry all the steps you have used, to reach the top, the load would soon crush you. Besides, there would be no steps for your brother to use as he follows on. Leave the steps for him to use if he chooses. They have assisted you to reach the top. You do not need them any longer. You may pause a moment for breath or for a fresh inspiration to go on. The moment that inspiration has come, you can place your foot upon the next step and again place the attainment in the storehouse. Let go of all the lessons that brought you there and there is nothing to encumber or hold you back. But, if you look back to the lessons and do not hold your vision on the goal, you will, before you realize it, have fixed the lessons instead of the ideal the lessons would convey.

"This may cause you to waver and look back and say, 'Did my ancestors accomplish in the way I have accomplished?' When I look far back I can say they did but, when I look into the immediate future I say they did not; for they accomplished by the sweat of their brow, while you are using your own God-given power. If you look back to your ancestors, you will, before you realize it, be worshipping them; for, with your creative ability you will have brought forth that which you have gazed upon. You will be living by their standards instead of your own. You will begin to look like your ancestors but you will not accomplish what they have accomplished. You will begin to drop back for, if you live by another's ideal, you cannot accomplish that which the one who conceived the ideal accomplished. You must either go on or return. There are no half-way measures. This ancestor worship is one of the direct causes of nations' degenerating. Because of your lack of ancestor worship we see a great nation in store for you. You had, in the first place, very little pride of ancestry; you had no ancestors to worship and you had no foundation save that which you made. Your ideal was a free country and you brought forth your ideal. The country you acquired had been free from king or ruler. To you it did not matter how your grandfather had accomplished. It was how you, your own individual self, would accomplish. Then, you united with the many to accomplish one purpose and the individual self in you, the creative power that gives you life (God), held you in direct communion with your ideal power to create. Then, with your eyes steadfastly fixed on the attainment, you are going on to the realization of your ideal."

Our hostess turned to the tablet and resumed, "On these tablets it is recorded that God was called Directive Principle — Head, Mind — and was symbolized by the character which is like your letter M, which was called M-o-o-h. This translated into your language would be *director* or *builder*.

"This Directive Principle was over all and controlled all. The first Being He created was called the expresssion of the Directive Principle; and He was created in form just like the Principle, as the Principle had no form but His own to express by or through. This Being which the Directive Principle created, was the outer expression of the Principle, Himself. He was created in the image of the Principle, as the Directive Principle had no other form to pattern after. The Directive Principle gave to His creation every one of His attributes and this creation had access to everything that the Principle had. He was given dominion over every outer form. He had the form of His Creator, the attributes of His Creator, and the power to express all of them in the perfect way that the Creator expresses, so long as the creation held itself in direct accord with the Principle. None of the attributes of the created being were developed but the Creator, having in mind the ideal or perfect plan which His creation was to express, placed His creation in ideal or perfect surroundings where all the attributes could be brought forth and expressed or brought into outer manifestation. Thus the Creator did not place His creation upon earth until all the conditions for its perfect development were complete. When these conditions were complete, this Being was placed among them and named Lord God and the location where He was placed was called M-o-o-h or M and afterward became known as the cradle or mother. I wish you to observe that I am putting this into words in your language so that you can understand them. You can go into the details later after you have learned to translate the tablets yourselves. I wish to bring these points out so that they may become the principle from which we shall work in translating these records. I do not wish you to think that I am attempting to change any conclusions you have already formed in other ways or through other thoughts or studies. I am going to ask you lay them all aside for the time. When you have gone deeper into these studies, you are at liberty to take up all others again, if you wish. I do not wish to influence you in any way. All lessons are but the outer, a way of arriving at a conclusion. If the conclusion is not reached or the aim sought is not attained, the lessons become driftwood, extra baggage, nothing."

CHAPTER III

DAY after day for two months, with the old man as our instructor, we gave our whole attention to a set of tablets which dealt entirely with characters, symbols, and their position, plan, and meaning. One morning early in March we went to the room in the temple, as usual, and found the old gentleman lying on the couch as though asleep. One of our party walked over and placed a hand on his arm to arouse him, then started back and exclaimed, "He is not breathing. I believe he is dead." We gathered around the couch and were so absorbed in our own thoughts of death among these people that we did not hear anyone enter. We were aroused from our reverie by a voice saying, "Good morning." We turned toward the door and there stood Emil. We had supposed that he was a thousand miles away and his sudden appearance had startled us. Before we had time to compose ourselves he had walked over and was shaking hands all around.

In a moment, Emil walked to the couch on which the old man was lying. Placing his hand upon the old man's head, he said, "Here we have a dear brother who has departed from this earth but has not been able to finish his work among us. As one of your poets has said, 'He has wrapped his mantle about him and has lain down to pleasant dreams.' In other words, you have pronounced him dead. Your first thought is to get an undertaker and a coffin, to prepare a grave to hide the mortal part of him while it dissolves.

"Dear friends, kindly think for a moment. To

whom did Jesus speak when he said, 'Father, I thank Thee that Thou hast heard me.' He was not talking to the outer self, the me, the shell. He was recognizing and praising the Inner Self, the One Infinite, the All Hearing, All Knowing, All Seeing, the Great and Mighty Omnipresent God. Can you not see where the eyes of Jesus were turned as he stood at the tomb of Lazarus? Did he, like you, look into that tomb and see a dead and dissolving Lazarus? While your vision was upon the dead, he held his vision upon the living, the only begotten of God. His vision was fixed upon unchangeable, eternal, omnipresent Life and that Life transcends all. Now, with our vision held steadfastly toward the ever-present reality of God, we can behold His finished work.

"Here is a dear brother who never relied wholly on God but went on partially in his own strength, until he has reached this stage and given up and made the mistake which so many are making today, the mistake you look upon as death. This dear soul has not been able to let go of all doubt and fear and thus he has relied on his own strength and has not been able to finish the work set before all. Should we leave him thus, his body will dissolve and he will be again sent forth to finish his mortal task, which is all but complete. In fact, so nearly complete is it that we can help him to finish and we feel this to be a great privilege.

"You asked if he can again be awakened to full consciousness. Yes, he can and so can all others who have similarly passed. Though he has passed, as you look upon it, we who have shared a part of his life with him can help and he will be able to understand quickly so that he may take his body with him. It is not necessary to leave the body to so-called death and dissolution even after one has apparently made the great mistake."

Here the speaker stopped and, for a moment, appeared to be lost in deep meditation. In a very short time four of our friends from the village walked into the room. They gathered close together for a few moments as though in deep thought. Then two of them reached out their hands and motioned us to join them. We stepped up close and two placed their arms around two of our party and we in turn placed our arms around each other until the circle was complete. The circle extended around the couch that the form of the departed was lying upon. As we stood there for a moment without a word being spoken, the light in the room became brighter. We turned and Jesus and Pilate were standing in the room together, a few steps away. They came forward and joined us.

There was another deep silence. Then Jesus stepped forward to the couch and, raising both hands, said, "Dear ones, will you just step through the vale of death with me for a moment? It is not forbidden ground as you think. If you will just step through as we have done and view it from the other side, you will see that it is only what your thoughts have made it. There is life there, the same life that is here." He stood for a moment with outstretched hands. "Dear friend and brother, you are with us and we are with you and we are all together with God. The sublime purity, peace, and harmony of God surrounds, embraces, and enriches all. This perfection now manifests so vividly to you, our dear one, that you may arise and be received unto your Father. Dear one, you see and know that it is not dust to dust and ashes to ashes, but it is Life, pure Life, Life Everlasting. Your body need not be left to mortal dissolution. You now perceive the glory of the Kingdom from which you come forth. You may now arise and go to your Father and the shout goes up, 'All hail, all hail, the new born one, the risen Lord, the Christ among men.' ''

Dear reader, words are but a travesty when the mortal attempts to picture the beauty and purity of the light that filled that room and, as that form arose, the light seemed to penetrate every object so that nothing cast a shadow, not even the form of our friend or our own bodies. The walls seemed to expand and become transparent until we seemed to be looking into infinite space. The glory of that picture cannot be told. Then we knew that, instead of standing in the presence of death, we were standing in the presence of Eternal Life, Life unspeakably grand, never diminishing but going on and on eternally.

What could we mortals do but stand and stare? In the uplift of those few moments we were carried, for a time, far beyond our most sanguine imagination of heaven and the beauty of it all. It was not a dream, but real. Thus the real can be greater than any dream. We were privileged to see through and beyond the shadow.

The beauty and tranquility of that scene and the great faith we had already placed in our friends carried us completely over the divide that day and today that divide is but a level plain. Yet in some way it was made clear that each one, for himself, must first scale the heights before the beauty beyond can be seen.

With every vestige of age gone, our friend, whom we looked upon as raised from the dead, turned toward his associates and, in a moment, began to speak. These are his words, as he stood facing our friends. It is as though they were cast in raised gold upon a tablet which stands always before me. The voice came forth with a majesty that I cannot express. There was no affectation, just a clear, deep note of sincerity and strength.

He said, "Dear ones, you cannot know the joy, the peace, the great bliss you have given me in awakening me as you have. Just a moment ago it was all dark; I stood, fearing to go on and yet I could not return. The only way that I can explain it is I seemed engulfed in a great blackness from which I suddenly seemed to awaken and now I am again with you." Here his face became so radiant with joy that there was no mistaking his sincerity.

Then he turned to us and said, "Dear ones, how I love to think of our association. You can never know the joy it has given me to have clasped your hands; the great joy it has given me to see and know and feel the sincerity with which you have accepted these, my dear helpers, who at this moment I am able to call divine. Could you see through my eyes at this moment, you would be able to know the bliss that I am experiencing. The greatest joy of all is to know so fully that each of you will stand and know, just as I am standing and knowing. That joy you will know only when you stand as I stand. I can say that it is well to have lived a full life, to be able to enjoy one moment of this. Then to think that I can see all eternity unfolding. Do you wonder when I say that my eyes are almost blinded and I am dazed with the revelation? Do you wonder at my great longing to unfold this vision to you, and not only to you, but to every brother and sister in the whole wide universe of God? Dear brothers, if I could lay a transforming hand upon you and lift you to where I stand, it seems that my joy would be multiplied manyfold at this moment. I am shown I must not do that. I am shown that you, yourselves, must stretch forth this transforming hand, and when you have stretched it forth you will find God's hand ready to clasp yours. You will be able to walk and talk with Him, and God will eternally bless you as He does all. The greatest joy of all is, I am shown that it does not matter what the caste or creed of church, all are welcome."

In a moment he had disappeared from our view, just faded away, it seemed to us. Was this an ethereal vision? All my associates concluded that it was not, for two of them had clasped this man's hand. I leave it to the reader to decide.

Then one of our friends from the village turned to us and said, "I know that you are doubting but won't you understand that this was not staged for your benefit? This is but one of the emergencies in our lives and, when the emergency does arise, we are able to come up over the emergency. This dear one had not been able in his own strength to quite surmount the divide, as you call it. In fact, as you see it, he had passed on. The soul had left the body behind and one so enlightened can be helped at the crucial moment, so that the soul returns and the body finishes its perfection; then the body can be taken along. This brother longed too ardently to pass on and he left his body when just a few more steps, as it were, helped it over the divide and the perfection was complete. The help extended was our great privilege."

We slowly withdrew our arms and stood for a full minute in absolute silence. One of our party broke the silence with the words, "My Lord and my God." As for me it did not seem as though I should ever want to talk again. I wanted to think.

We were all seated and a few had found their voices and were conversing in low tones. This condition had lasted for fifteen or twenty minutes and nearly everyone was engaged in general conversation, when one of our party walked to the window. He turned and said there seemed to be strangers arriving in the village. We all went down to meet them, as it was a very rare occurrence for strangers to visit the village at this season of the year and on foot, as it was just past midwinter.

When we arrived, we found that it was a party from a smaller village about thirty miles down the valley. They had brought a man who had lost his way in a storm three days previous and had been nearly frozen. His friends had carried him on a stretcher all that distance through the snow. Jesus stepped close and, placing his hand upon the man's head, stood for a moment. Almost instantly the man threw off the wrappings and rose to his feet. His friends, when they saw him stand, stared at him for an instant, then ran from the scene in terror. We could not persuade them to return. The man who was healed seemed dazed and uncertain. Two of our friends persuaded him to go with them to their homes, while our party, accompanied by Jesus, returned to our quarters.

CHAPTER IV

A FTER we were comfortably seated, Jesus proceeded with the conversation.

"When we stand one with the sum of all Intelligence, and recognize ourselves as an actual part of that Intelligence, and know conclusively that this is the Great Principle, God, we shall soon find ourselves conscious of the fact that all intelligence throughout the whole cosmic Universe is working with us. We also realize quickly that the intelligence of all great genius, as well as the little mentality of the single cell of the body, is working with us in perfect harmony and accord. This is the One Great Intelligent Cosmic Mind that we are positively allied with. Indeed, we are that very Mind; we are the self-consciousness of the Universe. The instant we feel this very thing, nothing can keep us from the Godhead.

"From this Universal Consciousness we can draw all knowledge; we know that we can know all, without studying and without process of reasoning, not going from one lesson to another nor from one point to another. The lessons are necessary only in order to bring us to the attitude in which we can step forth into this thought. Then we become comprehensive and include all thought. There is a complete stream of motivating thought that is irresistible and we know that nothing can divert us from true accomplishment. We are with the whole; thus we move on irresistibly with the whole. It is impossible for any condition to keep us from our accomplishment. The drop of water is only weak when it is removed from the ocean; replace it and it is as powerful as the whole ocean. It matters not whether we like it or whether we believe it. It is Intelligent Law and we are that very thing.

"The sum of all Truth is the Great Principle, God. Everything from Eternity to Eternity, whether we think it is a great truth or a little truth; every true word, thought or spoken; is a part of The Great Truth, One Great All, One Universal Truth, and we are that very thing. When we realize this oneness and stand absolutely with Truth, we have the whole of Truth back of us and our irresistibility is increased. It is the force of the ocean back of the wave that gives the wave its power; that, too, is but a portion of God-force which man also is.

"The sum of all Love is the Great Principle, God. It is the sum of every affection, every fervent emotion, every loving thought, look, word, or deed. Every attracted love, great or small, sublime or low, makes the one infinite love stand forth and nothing is too great for us. As we love unselfishly, we have the complete ocean of Cosmic Love with us. That which is thought least is greatest as it sweeps on to absolute perfection; thus the whole Universe of Love is consciously with us. There is no greater power on earth or in heaven than pure love. Earth becomes heaven; heaven is Humanity's true home.

"Finally, the sum of every condition, every form, every being is the One Infinite Cosmic Principle, God, whether it be individuals, worlds, planets, stars, atoms, electrons, or the most minute particles. All together make One Infinite Whole, the body of which is the Universe, the Mind, Cosmic Intelligence; the soul, Cosmic Love. Woven together as a whole, their bodies, minds, and souls are held together with the cohesive force of love; yet each one functions in eternal individual identity, moving freely in its individual orbit and octave of harmony, attracted, drawn, and held together by the love of that universe of harmony. We constitute that Great Being that nothing can thwart. It is made up of every unit of humanity as well as every unit of the Universe. If a portion of one unit excludes itself from the whole, it makes no difference to Principle Being but it makes a vast difference to the unit. The ocean is not conscious of the removal of the drop of water but the drop is very conscious of the ocean when it is returned or reunited with it.

"It is not enough for us to say that we are close to the Great Cosmic Principle, God. We must know definitely that we are one with, in, and of, and amalgamated entirely with, Principle; and that we can not be separated or apart from God, Principle. Thus we work with the principle of power which is all power. It is the Law that in Principle we live, move, and have our being. Thus, when we wish to come in contact with God, we do not think of something away from us and difficult to attain. All we need know is that God is within as well as all about us and that we are completely included in God; that we are consciously within the presence of God and are present in God and in command with full power. Thus we need not pause, we need not ponder; we take the path directly to God within. Here the Christ stands steadfast and supreme and with God we endure forever.

"Thus we arouse our dead selves into the realization of the life within and that life resurrects us from the dead; we return to life immortal, unchanging. We are convinced of life and of our right to live that life fully and perfectly. The Christ within stands forth and says, 'I come that you may have complete life and live that more abundantly.' This must be a true resurrection in our consciousness — an uplifting of our dead senses into a higher vibration of life, truth, and love. As all nature is awakening about us, let us arouse ourselves and see the dawn of this approaching day. Thus, we get up and out of our grave clothes, up and out of all sense of limitation in which we have bound our bodies. We roll the stone of materiality completely from our consciousness, that heavy weight of thought that has separated the life within from the life without; and which has held the life form in death and denied it life because we have not recognized its right to life. Let us get up and out of death — that is what the resurrection means. It is an awakening to the full realization of life here and now — and that life omnipresent, omnipotent, omniscient; nowhere absent, nowhere powerless, nowhere unconscious; but everywhere present, everywhere powerful, everywhere conscious, in fullness, in freedom, in gloriously radiant expressive, expanding action. When our hearts flame to this thought and our whole being glows with this life within, we can readily extend our hand and say 'Lazarus, come forth! Get out of your grave, you do not belong in death! Come to life! Awake from your delusion! Awake now and here.' Thus we are awakened to the Master consciousness and we shall weep because of the density of thought of those that watch the awakening. Thousands of years of this awakening have been presented to humanity, yet many sleep. But their sleeping does not justify us in doing so. It is because of what we do that humanity is awakened to that rightful heritage.

"As we awaken to our rightful heritage, we shall awaken to the beauty and purity of the age-old message that our bodies are eternally beautiful, pure and perfect. They are always beautiful, pure, spiritual bodies, most magnificent and divine, the true temples of God. This awakening also convinces us that our bodies have never descended from that high estate. We see that it was only a human concept

46

wherein we thought they had descended. As soon as this thought is released, our body is released to its true inheritance of divinity. Then the fragrance of a warm summer evening suffuses all nature and our bodies begin to take on this effulgence. Soon pure rays of white light appear within our bodies; they become aglow with this light; and this soft, yet brilliant, living light invades the clear atmosphere around us like a white-gold vapor. This light increases steadily until it covers and permeates everything about us. Bathed in this radiance, there appears a pure crystal white light, dazzling and scintillating with a radiance greater than that of the purest diamond, yet it is emanating from our bodies and they stand forth ablaze with pure light, radiant and beautiful. Here we stand together on the Holy Mount of Transfiguration, with bodies luminous and glowing, radiant and beautiful, immersed wholly in Divine Life. The Son of man has become the Christ of God and the Kingdom of God is once more among mankind and more vital because others have accepted and brought forth the Kingdom in full dominion. The light of the God Kingdom grows stronger because of the acceptance.

"This is the true body which Humanity has always had and which all have today. Such a body always has existed and always will exist. It is a body so luminous that no germ of old age or decay can find lodgement therein. It is a body so alive that it can not die. Such a body can be crucified a thousand times and, because of such a crucifixion, come forth more triumphant. Such a body stands forth as the Divine Master of every situation. Such a body is eternally resurrected.

"This is a new-age message to you, the same as it seemed to be a new-age message two thousand years ago. It is the same today as it was then; it is but the

THE LIFE OF THE MASTERS OF THE FAR EAST

resurrection of the age-old message. This message was told thousands of centuries ago in language so simple that babes could read. The message is that man of his own free will shall leave the man-made kingdom and evolve to the God Kingdom. The son of man is to realize his divinity, reveal this divinity in his body and affairs, and become the Christ of God in the Kingdom of God. 'Know ye not that ye are gods?'

"Within you, know that this Kingdom of God is the most natural thing in the world. You have but overlooked the fact that if man be in Christ he is a new creature. 'It is the Father's good pleasure to give you the kingdom, and every man passeth into it.' The question is asked 'When?' The answer always is, 'When the without is as the within.'

"The great oak tree that sleeps within the acorn became aroused throughout the whole acorn before the tree could develop. 'Eye hath not seen, nor ear heard, nor hath it entered into the heart of man to conceive of the things that God hath prepared for them that love him.'

"God knows that in the great structure of the universe there is a splendid place for every human being and that each has his individual place. The structure can stand only because each is in his right place. Does not this message lighten the burden of everyone and adorn each countenance with a smile, even those of the weary ones who think they labor like dumb, driven cattle? Thus I say to you, you are an especially designed creation, you have a particular mission, you have a light to give, a work to do that no other can give or accomplish; and if you will open your heart, mind, and soul wide to spirit, you will learn of it in your own heart. There you find that your very own Father speaks to you. No matter

how wayward or thoughtless you have thought yourself, you will find that your Father loves you devo-
tedly and tenderly the instant you turn to God within. The anointing which you have of God abides in
you and you need not the teaching of any man. Is
this not a resurrection from the old thought? 'Ye
need not that any man teach you.' It is only necessary to receive the anointing from God that has always been yours. You may accept others as brother
helpers but you are always instructed and led from
within; the truth is there for you and you will find it.

"That truth always teaches that humanity is a
complete unit; not a unity, but a great unit; combined with God they are the Great One. Humanity is
more than a brotherhood. It is One Man, just as a
vine and its branches are one vine. No one part or
one unit can be separated from the whole. The
Christ's prayer is 'That they all may be One.'

" 'He that hath done it unto the least of these my
brethren, hath done it unto me.' Now you know the
Christ for whom the whole family in heaven and on
earth is named.

"The Truth is, 'All is One'; One Spirit, One Body,
the Great Lord Body of all humanity. The Great
Love, Light, Life of God completely amalgamates
that body into One Complete Whole."

CHAPTER V

AT ONE time, conversation led on to a point where one of our party asked where hell was and what the devil meant. Jesus turned quickly and said, "Hell or the devil has no abiding place except in man's mortal thought. Both of them are just wherever man places them. With your present enlightenment, can you place either in any geographical position on earth? If heaven is all and surrounds all, where could hell or the devil be placed ethereally? If God rules all and is All, where could either be placed in God's perfect plan?

"If we take the science of things, we know there is a legend told here that all the heat and light and many other natural forces are contained right within the earth itself. The sun, of itself, has no heat or light. It has potentialities that draw the heat and light from the earth. After the sun has drawn the heat and light rays from the earth, the heat rays are reflected back to the earth by the atmosphere that floats in the ether. The light rays are drawn from the earth in about the same manner and are reflected back to the earth by the ether. As the air extends only a comparatively short distance, the effect of the heat rays varies as you leave the earth's surface and ascend toward the outer limit of the atmosphere. As the air becomes less dense, there is less reflection; consequently as you ascend into the higher altitudes the heat becomes less and the cold increases. Every heat ray, as it is drawn out and reflected, drops back to the earth, where it is regenerated. When you have reached the limit of air, you have reached the limit of heat. It is the same with the light rays. They are drawn from the earth and reflected back by the ether. As this ether extends much farther from the earth than the air, the light rays extend much farther before they are all reflected. When you have reached the limit of ether, you have reached the limit of light. When you have reached the limit of heat and light, you have reached the great cold. This cold is far more solid than steel, and it presses down upon the ether and the atmosphere with almost irresistible force and holds them together. Hell is supposed to be warm and his Satanic Majesty abhors cold; so you could not find any lodging place out there for them.

"Now that we have disposed of them above, let us take the other scientific legend and go below. According to this legend, the earth a short distance from the surface is a molten mass. It is so hot that it will melt any substance. This molten mass at the center revolves more slowly than does the crust at the outer, and the belt where the two meet is the place where the natural forces are generated and there, again, the hand of God rules all. So there is no place for His Satanic Majesty or his home there; for, if he attempted to live in either the hottest or the coldest place, he would find it very uncomfortable, since cold will consume as well as heat. We have searched every place and we can not find him a home; so we must assume that he is right where man is and has all the power that man gives him.

"It was only the personal adversary that I cast out. Do you think for a moment that I would cast the devil out of any man and then allow him to enter a heard of swine that cast themselves into the sea? I never saw the devil in any man, save he brought him there himself. The only dominion I ever gave him was that which man himself gave him."

Later the talk led to God and one of our party

51

said, "I would like to know who or what God really is." Then Jesus spoke and said, "I believe that I understand the motive of the question you would like to clear up in your own mind. It is the many conflicting thoughts and ideas that are puzzling or disturbing the world today without reference to the origin of the word. God is the principle behind everything that exists today. The principle behind a thing is Spirit; and Spirit is Omnipotent, Omnipresent, Omniscient. God is the one Mind that is both the direct and the directing cause of all the good that we see about us. God is the source of all the true Love that holds or binds all forms together. God is impersonal principle. God is never personal except as He becomes to each individual a personal loving Father-Mother. To the individual He can be a personal, loving, all-giving Father-Mother. God never becomes a great being located somewhere in the skies in a place called heaven, where He has a throne which He sits upon and judges people after they die; for God is the Life itself and that life never dies. That is but a misconception brought about by man's ignorant thinking, just as so many malformations have been brought about and you see them in the world around you. God is not a judge or a king who can intrude His presence upon you or bring you before the bar of justice. God is a loving, all-giving Father-Mother, who, when you approach, puts out His arms and enfolds you. It does not matter who or what you are or what you have been. You are His child just the same as when you seek Him with a true heart and purpose. If you are the Prodigal Son who has turned his face from the Father's house and you are weary of the husks of life that you are feeding to the swine, you can again turn your face to the Father's house and be certain of a loving welcome. The feast ever awaits you there. The table is always spread, and when you do return, there will not be a reproach from a brother that has returned before you.

"God's love is like a pure spring that gushes from a mountain. At its source it is pure but as it flows on its course it becomes clouded and polluted until it enters the ocean so impure it does not even resemble that which emerged from the source. As it enters the ocean it begins to drop the mud and slime to the bottom and again rises to the surface as a part of the glad, free ocean, from which it again can be taken up to refresh the spring.

"You can see and talk with God at any time, just as you can with father, mother, brother, or friend. Indeed, He is far closer than any mortal can be. God is far dearer and truer than any friend. God is never wrought up, nor angry, nor cast down. God never destroys, nor hurts, nor hinders one of His children or creatures or creations. If God did these things, He would not be God. The god that judges, destroys, or withholds any good thing from his children or creatures or creations is but a god that is conjured up by man's ignorant thinking; and you need not fear that god unless you wish to do so. For the true God stretches forth His hand and says, 'All that I have is yours.' When one of your poets said that God is closer than breathing and nearer than hands or feet, he was inspired by God. All are inspired by God when that inspiration is for the good or the right and all can be inspired by God at all times if they only will.

"When I said, 'I am the Christ, the only begotten of God', I did not declare this for myself alone, for had I done this I could not have become the Christ. I say definitely that, in order to bring forth the Christ, I, as well as all others, must declare it; then must live the life, and the Christ must appear. You may declare the Christ all you will and, if you do not live the life, the Christ will never appear. Just think, dear friends, if all would declare the Christ then live the life for one year or five years, what an awakening there would be. The possibilities cannot be imagined. That was the vision that I saw. Dear ones, can you not place yourselves where I stood and see as I saw? Why do you surround me with the murk and mire of superstition! Why do you not lift your eyes and minds and thoughts above these and see with a clear vision! Then you would see that there are no miracles, no mysteries, no pain, no imperfection, no inharmony, and no death, except that which man has made. When I said 'I have overcome death,' I knew wherof I spoke; but it took the crucifixion to show these dear ones.

"There are a great many of us joined together to help the whole world and this is our lifework. There have been times when it has taken our combined energies to ward off the evil thoughts, of doubt and disbelief and superstition that have nearly engulfed mankind. You may call them evil forces if you wish. We know that they are evil only as man makes them so. But now we see the light growing brighter and brighter as the dear ones throw off the bonds. The throwing off of these bonds may for a time sink mankind into materiality; but even so, it is a step nearer the goal, for materiality does not hold one as superstition and myth and mystery hold one. When I stepped upon the water that day, do you think that I cast my eyes downward into the great depths, the material substance? No, I fastened my eyes steadfastly on God Power that transcends any power of the deep. The moment I did this the water became as firm as a rock and I could walk upon it in perfect safety."

Jesus stopped talking for a moment, and one of

our party asked, "While we are talking, does it not hinder you from going right on with your work?"

Jesus answered and said, "You cannot hinder one of our friends here for a moment and I believe I am included as one of them."

Someone spoke and said, "You are our Brother." Then Jesus' face lighted up with a smile as he said, "Thank you, I have always named you Brothers."

One of the party then turned and asked Jesus, "Can all bring forth the Christ?" He answered, "Yes, there is but one end of accomplishment. Man came forth from God and he must return to God. That which from the heavens descended must again ascend unto heaven. The history of the Christ did not begin with my birth; neither did it end with the crucifixion. The Christ was when God created the first man in His own image and likeness. The Christ and that man are one; all men and that man are one. As God was his Father, so is He the father of all men and all are God's children. As the child has the quality of the parents, so the Christ is in every child. For many years the child lived and realized his Christhood, his oneness with God, through the Christ in himself. Then began the history of the Christ and you can trace this history back to man's beginning. That the Christ means more than the man Jesus goes without contradiction. Had I not perceived this, I could not have brought forth the Christ. To me this is the pearl without price, the old wine in new bottles, the truth which many others have brought forth and thus have fulfilled the ideals that I have fulfilled and proved.

"For more than fifty years after that day on the cross I taught and lived with my disciples and many of those I loved dearly. In those days we gathered at a quiet place outside Judea. There we were free from the prying eyes of superstition. There many acquired the great gifts and they accomplished a great work. Then, seeing that, by withdrawing for a time, I would be able to reach and help all, I withdrew. Besides, they were depending upon me instead of upon themselves; and, in order to make them self-reliant, it was necessary for me to withdraw from them. If they had lived in close association with me, then could they not find me again if they desired to do so?

"The cross was, in the beginning, the symbol of the greatest joy the world ever knew. The foundation of the cross is the place where man first trod the earth, therefore the mark that symbolizes the dawn of a celestial day here on earth. If you will trace it back, you will find that the cross disappears entirely and that it is the man standing in the attitude of devotion, standing in space with arms upraised in blessing, sending out his gifts to humanity, pouring all his gifts forth freely in every direction.

"When you know that the Christ is the fitting life within the form, the rising energy that the scientist glimpses, yet does not know whence it came; when you feel with the Christ that the life is lived so that life may be given freely; when you learn that man is obliged to live by the constant dissolution of forms, and that the Christ lived to give up the thing that the body of sense craved, for the good that he could not at the moment enjoy — you are the Christ. When you see yourself a part of the greater life but willing to sacrifice yourself for the good of the whole; when you learn to do right without being affected by the outcome to help; when you learn freely to give up physical life and all that the world has to give (this is not self-abnegation or poverty, for as you give of God you will find you have the more to give, although at times duty may seem to demand all that life has to give. You will also know that he who will save his life shall lose it) then you will see that the pure gold is at the deepest part of the furnace where the fire has fully cleansed it. You will find great joy in knowing that the life you have given to others is the life you have won. You will know that to receive is to give freely; that, if you lay down the mortal form, a higher life will prevail. You have the glad assurance that a life thus won is won for all.

"You must know that the Great Christ Soul can go down to the river and that the stepping into the water but typifies the sympathy you feel for the world's great need. Then you are able to help your fellow-men and not boast of virtue; you can pass out the bread of life for the hungry souls that come to you, yet that bread never diminishes by the giving; you must press on and know fully that you are able to heal all that come to you, sick or weary or heavy laden, with the Word that makes whole the soul; you are able to open the eyes of those blinded either from ignorance or from choice. (It does not matter how low the blinded soul may be, he must feel that the Christ soul stands beside him and he must find that you tread with human feet the very ground he treads. Then you will know that the true Unity of Father and Son is within and not without. You will know that you must stand serene when the God without is put away and only the God within remains. You must be able to withhold the cry of love and fear as the words, 'My God, my God, why have you forsaken me?' ring out. Still, at that hour you must not feel alone for you must know that you stand with God; that you are nearer to the heart of the loving Father than you have ever been before. You must know that the hour you touch the deepest sorrow is the hour in which your greatest triumph begins. With all this you must know that sorrows cannot touch you.

"From that hour your voice will ring with a great, free song, for you fully know that you are the Christ, this light which is to shine among men and for men. Then you will know the darkness that is in every soul that cannot find a helping hand to clasp as he journeys on the rugged road before he finds the Christ within.

"You must know that you are truly divine and, being divine, you must see that all men are as you are. You will know that there are dark places you must pass with the light that you are to carry to the highest and your soul will ring out in praise that you can be of service to all men. Then, with a glad free shout, you mount to your very highest in your union with God.

"Now you know that there is no substitution of your life for other lives or of your purity for others' sins; but that all are glad, free spirits in and of themselves and of God. You know that you can reach them while they cannot reach each other; that you cannot help giving of your life for the life of each soul, that it shall not perish. Yet you must be so reverent of that soul that you will not pour into it a flood of life unless the life of that soul opens to receive it. But you will freely pour out to it a flood of love, life, and light, so that when that one does open the windows the light of God will pour in and illuminate him. You will know that in every Christ that arises, humanity is lifted one step higher. Then, too, you must know full well that you have everything that the Father has; and having all, it is for all to use. You must know that as you rise and are true, you lift the whole world with you; for as you tread the path it becomes plainer for your fellow-men. You must have faith in yourself, knowing fully that that faith is God within. Finally, you must know that you are a temple of God, a house not made with hands, immortal in the earth and in heaven as well.

"Then will they sing of you, 'All Hail, All Hail, He comes, He comes, the King; and lo, He is with you always. You are in God and He is in you.'"

Jesus arose, saying he would be obliged to leave us, as he was to be at the home of another Brother in the same village that evening. The whole company arose. Jesus blessed all and, with two of the gathering, walked from the room.

CHAPTER VI

AFTER we were again seated, one of our party turned to Emil and asked if all could acquire the art of healing. He said, "The power to heal can be obtained only as we learn to trace things out from their source. Supremacy over every discord can come only in the degree that we understand that they do not come from God.

"The divinity that shapes your destinies is not a mighty person molding you as a potter molds his clay but a Mighty Divine Power—within and all around you and around and in all substance—which is yours to use as you will. If you do not realize this, you cannot have confidence in yourselves. The greatest cure for inharmony is the knowledge that it is not from God and that God never did create it.

"The brain has the quality of receiving and recording the vibrations of any object that the eye conveys to it. The vibrations of the lights and shades and colors are all recorded. It also has the quality of reproducing these vibrations and projecting them out again, this time through the inner vision; then we again see the picture the eye has conveyed. You are reproducing this in your camera every time you expose a sensitized plate. That plate receives and records the vibrations that the object you wish to photograph sends out. After the vibrations are received and recorded on the plate, you must fix the results on the plate, if they are to become permanent so that you can see them. It will be only a short time before you will find that the movements and colors of the objects that you photograph can be recorded and projected by first fixing and then returning or projecting the lights and colors at the same rate of vibration at which they were received and fixed.

"It is the same with thought and word and act. Each selective set of brain cells takes up and records its corresponding set of vibrations and, when these vibrations are repeated and projected, they can be reproduced just as they took place, if the cells are held directly to their duty.

"There is also another set of selective brain cells that can receive, record, and fix the vibrations of the thoughts, acts, motions, and pictures that other bodies or forms send out. These vibrations can be again reproduced and projected and you can so arrange these cells that you can reproduce the words and motions of these bodies or objects and even the thoughts of those that send them out. Through these cells you can assist others as well as yourself to control their thoughts. It is through these cells that accidents and calamities are brought about, such as wars, earthquakes, floods, fires and all the trouble that mortal man is heir to. Someone either sees a thing happen or images it as happening; the corresponding vibration is fixed in the cells, sent out to be impressed on the corresponding cells of other brains, then again projected back, until the thing is so fixed that it happens.

"All these things can be avoided if the thought that sustains them is immediately withdrawn and the vibrations are not allowed to be fixed upon those brain cells, so that those particular vibrations cannot be again projected. It is through this set of cells that all calamities are foretold.

"There is still another set of selective brain cells that receive, record, and fix the vibrations of the thoughts and activities of Divine Mind, wherein all the true vibrations are created and sent out. This Divine Mind, or God, pervades every substance and

61

is always sending out divine and true vibrations and, if we hold these cells to their true office, we are able to receive and send out the same true and divine vibrations that we receive from Divine Mind. We do not have the Divine Mind but we have the cells that receive and project the vibrations of the Divine Mind."

There was a pause and deep silence, then a picture appeared upon the wall of the room. It was still at first but, in a moment, it became animated and, after the lapse of another moment, the scene began to change. Scenes that could represent those enacted in any or all of the more prosperous business centers of the world came flooding in. While they were changing very rapidly, there was sufficient time for us to recognize and name many familiar places; and one in particular, a reproduction of the scenes enacted when we landed in Calcutta in December, 1894. This was long before we had evern heard of the cinema or motion picture. Yet these pictures depicted and brought out all the movements of the human form and other objects. These pictures continued to pour in at intervals of about one minute's duration, for nearly an hour.

While these pictures were passing, Emil said, "These pictures represent the conditions that exist in the world today. You will note the air of general peace and prosperity that prevails over a greater portion of the earth. There is a reasonable amount of contentment; the people seem undisturbed and generally happy. But underneath, there is a seething caldron of discord, generated by man's own ignorant thinking. There is hate, intrigue, and discord among nations. Men are beginning to visualize great military establishments, the like of which were never before known on earth. While we are doing everything in our power to bring out the good, our combined efforts will not be sufficient to sway those who are determined to rule in their own might. If they are able to perfect and launch their diabolical plans — and this we fully expect they will do, for people and nations are sleeping just when they should be awake and thinking — within a few years you will see enacted pictures like these." Then ten or twelve war scenes came trooping by. They were scenes that we never dreamed could actually take place and we gave them but little thought. Emil continued, "We are hoping almost against hope that these can be averted. Time will tell and these conditions are what we are hoping will prevail." Then scenes of beauty and peace beyond all description came trooping past, and Emil said, "These are scenes which all of you will see enacted but we wish you would, in so far as possible, put the second series of pictures out of your minds, as that will help us more than you think."

After a short pause one of our party asked what the words "Lord God" implied, and Emil continued. "The 'Lord God' was used to designate the Perfect Being that the Divine Principle, or God, created to bring out His qualities here on earth. This Being was created in the image and likeness of the Divine Principle and had access to, and could use, everything that the Divine Principle had. This Being was given power and dominion over every condition that existed upon the earth. This Being had all the potentialities of the Divine Principle and the power to bring them forth as long as He cooperated with the Divine Principle and developed the faculties that had been given Him, in the ideal way that the Divine Principle had planned or was holding in mind. This Being was afterwards called 'Lord God,' which meant expression in creative action or the Law of God. This is the Perfect Being that the Divine Principle holds in mind for man to express. This is the Divine and Only Man that the Divine Principle created. Man, or the spiritual side of his nature, has access to and can become this Lord God or One Man. This Divine Man afterwards became known as the Christ. He had dominion over heaven and earth and all things therein. Then the Lord God, using His power to create, did create other beings like unto Himself. These beings were afterwards called sons of the Lord God and their Creator was called Father and the Divine Principle was called God."

Here he paused for a moment and held out his hand and almost immediately there was in it a large piece of plastic substance that resembled clay. This he placed on the table and began molding it into a form which afterwards took on the image of a beautiful human figure about six inches in height. So deftly did he work that the image was finished in a very short time. After it was finished, he held it in both hands for a moment; then he held it up and breathed upon it and it became animated. He held it in his hands for a moment longer, then placed it on the table, where it moved about. It acted so much like a human being that we never asked a question but stood with our mouths and eyes wide open and stared.

Emil spoke, quoting, " 'And the Lord God created man from the dust of the ground and breathed into his nostrils the breath of life and he became a living soul.' Then sons of the Lord God created man from the dust of the ground; and they, with their creative ability, breathed the breath of life into the statue and it became a living soul. The genius can do this with his pottery or handiwork. If he leaves the statue or picture as his hands form it, it is an image and he has no responsibility; but if he goes on and uses his creative power to put life into it, his responsibility never ceases. He must keep watch of each of his creations and they must be held in divine order. This is where man in one way lost contact with God. He made images like these; then he did not withdraw the life which he, in his ardor, had endowed them with and they wandered over the earth without purpose or aim. Whereas, had he withdrawn the life he had endowed them with, there would have been but the statue and his responsibility would have ceased."

Here the image stopped moving and Emil continued, "You have seen the clay in the hands of the potter but it is man, not God, that is manipulating the clay. Had he created it from God's pure substance as he was created, it, like him, would have been a pure and true son. This will be much clearer to you after you have translated the first series of tablets. As it is late I think you would like to retire."

As soon as the last guest had departed, we prepared to retire, feeling that the last few days had been filled to overflowing.

CHAPTER VII

THE next morning we took up the regular work of translating, in order to get as clear an insight as possible into the meaning of the characters employed in compiling the records. In fact, we were learning the alphabet of this ancient writing. In this we became very deeply engrossed, with our hostess as teacher.

We had been occupied in this work for about two weeks when we went to the temple one morning and found our friend Chander Sen, who had apparently died and been resurrected, with not a vestige of old age about him. There was no mistaking him. As we came into the room he arose and came forward with a hearty greeting and handshake. You can imagine our surprise as we gathered around and began to ask questions. We were like a gang of schoolboys turned loose, all attempting to ask questions at the same time. But the fact remained, there he was, with the unmistakable form and voice but with not a trace of old age about him. Even the voice had regained the vibrant quality of middle age and everything about him showed the quality of a well-developed life, buoyant and keenly alive. The expression of the eyes and face was far beyond anything that I could put into words.

In the first few moments we could do nothing but picture to ourselves the contrast. When we had first seen him, he was a decrepit old man, leaning on a long staff for support, with long snow-white locks, halting step, and emaciated form. One of our party had remarked when we first met him, "Here we find among these great souls one so aged that he seems ready to pass to the great beyond." Of course, the transformation which we had witnessed just a few days previous had left its impression, but his sudden disappearance had rather taken him and the incident out of our minds, as we did not think we would ever see him again. It was more than a rejuvenation. I can compare it only to the transfiguration of the One we love and respect so dearly. That soul was surely reborn, judging from the contrast between his appearance the first time we met him and the way he looked this morning. It is true that we had known him only a short time but we had been thrown in daily contact with him for a sufficient time to see and know that he was an old man. He was with us for nearly two years after this, acting as our guide and interpreter across the great Gobi. Years after, when two or three of the party would meet and our experiences were recalled, the experience of that morning would be the first subject brought up.

In recounting these events, I am not going to attempt to follow our whole conversation and record it word for word, for we consumed the greater part of two days in just talking and I believe a detailed account would be tedious reading. Therefore, in this instance I shall bring out only the main points.

After the first excitement had abated somewhat, we were seated and he began, "As the body represents the lowest degree of thought activities, so the Spirit represents the highest thoughts of Divine Mind. As the body is the outer expression of the thought, so the Spirit is that in which the form takes its initial impulse direct from the Divine Mind. It is the immortal and real Self, in which reside all the potentialities of Divine Mind.

"The thought atmosphere is a real, substantial

thing and has in it all that makes the body. So many people consider the things that they cannot see as unsubstantial; and although they are told, over and over that they cannot conceal themselves, they go right on believing that they can. Did Adam and Eve conceal themselves when they were hiding from the Lord, or Law of God? It is well for us to know the truth that we carry around with us the open book of our lives, out of which all men read whether we realize it or not. Some people are good thought readers, while others are dull; but all can read a little and we cannot conceal ourselves. Also, our thought atmosphere is constantly precipitating its slowly cooling words on our body and there it is seen by all men. We can, with a little practice, feel the thought force of this atmosphere that surrounds us and gradually gain a realization of its existence as real as that of the outer world.

"I have learned that just as man may touch the earth with his feet, so on the wings of aspiration may he soar to celestial heights. Like those of old, he may walk the earth and talk with God and the more he does so, the more difficult it will be for him to discover where Universal Life ends and where individual existence begins. When man forms an alliance with God through spiritual understanding, the boundary line between God and man disappears. When this point is reached, man will know what Jesus meant when He said, 'I and my Father are one.'

"The great philosophers through the ages have accepted the idea of man as a trinity but it never was their belief that he has a triple personality. They have considered him a being who in his nature is triune.

"The tendency to personalize all things has de-

68

graded that which is called the Blessed Trinity into the impossible conception of three in one, when it can be best understood as the Omnipresence, Omnipotence, Omniscience of the Universal Mind, God. As long as men consider the Blessed Trinity as three persons in one and as something that must be accepted even though it cannot be explained, they will dwell in the wilderness of superstition and thus, of doubt and fear.

"If the triune nature of God is spiritual rather than physical, then the trinity in man must be seen from a mental rather than from a material point of view. One of the wise philosophers has said, "Despising everything else, a wise man should strive after a knowledge of Self, for there is no knowledge that is higher, or that brings more satisfaction of power, than a knowledge of his own being.' If a man knows his real Self, he cannot do otherwise than discover his latent possibilities, his concealed powers, his dormant faculties. Of what avail, if a man should 'gain the whole world and lose his own soul?' His soul is his spiritual self and, if he truly discovers his spiritual self, he can build a whole world if he is serving his fellow-men by so doing. I have learned that he who would attain the ultimate goal must search the depths of his real Self and there he will find God, the fullness of all good. It is because man is a trinity in unity — composed of spirit, soul, and body — that, in a state of spiritual ignorance, he has the tendency to think on a level with the lowest degree of his nature, which is the physical.

"The ignorant man looks to his body for all the pleasure he gets and there comes a time when he gets from the senses all the pain that he can stand. What he does not learn through wisdom he must learn through woe and, after repeated experiences, he will not deny that wisdom is the better way. Jesus, Osiris, and Buddha said that with all our understanding, we must get wisdom.

"Thought, operating on the plane of the intellectual, raises the vibrations of the body to a point which corresponds to liquid. On this plane, thought is neither wholly material nor wholly spiritual. It is vibrating like a pendulum between materiality and spirituality but there comes a time when one must choose which one he will serve. If he chooses materiality, a world of confusion and chaos awaits him. He may choose the spirit and, if he does so choose, he may ascend to the dome of the temple of God in man. This state of thought can be compared to the gaseous in matter, which is elastic and tends to expand indefinitely. God always leaves it for man to say whether he will control his fluidic stream of thought in the direction of those celestial heights which bear him above the fog line of doubt, fear, sin, and sickness or let it sink to the sordid depths of the animal in man.

"If, in thinking of man as a trinity of spirit, mind, and body, we consider him principally from the standpoint of mind, or soul, we shall see that he occupies a position between two great extremes of mental activity, the lower of which is the body, and the higher, the spirit. Mind is the connecting link between the visible and invisible. Operating on the plane of the senses, the mind becomes the seat of all the animal appetites and passions. It is the serpent in man's Garden of Eden which beguiles him into partaking of the poisoned fruit. When Jesus said, 'As Moses lifted up the serpent in the wilderness, even so must the son of man be lifted up,' he was not referring to the raising of his body on the cross but to the elevation of the soul or mind above sense delusions. Standing between spirit and body, though separated from neither, the soul or mind is capable of thinking even lower than the brute thinks; or it may enter into conscious union with pure spirit where there is an abundance of peace, purity, and God Power.

"When the son of man is lifted up to that realm in which he rises above the fallacies of the physical realm, he thinks and acts on the plane of pure intelligence. There he discriminates between those instincts which he shares with every other animal and those divine intuitions which he has in common with God. I have been shown that when man thinks on a plane with pure spirit, the soul enters consciously that realm wherein it perceives the ideal of things, rather than the things themselves. It is no longer dependent upon the senses but, with clearer vision, it sees the broad horizon's grander view. It is here that truth is revealed by Divine Intelligence and speaks the inspiring and health-giving message.

"When the son of man has been lifted from the depth of his material world and has been surrounded by pictures of tranquil beauty and refinement of the mental world, after a time he is seized with a healthy dissatisfaction and the ever-upward urge of the soul bears him to higher realms. There he no longer sees the pictures of tranquillity but dwells in the land of tranquillity, surrounded by perpetual beauty. He has glimpsed the inner and to him that has become the all; and the outer has become the inner. He lives in a world of causes where before he moved in a world of effects.

"The spirit of triune man is pure intelligence, that region of his being where neither sense testimony nor human opinion has any weight against ascertained truth; it is the Christ within, or the Son of God in the son of man, the discovery of which sets at rest doubt and its discouragements. It is from this pinnacle of his being that man views all things with

71

the clear vision of the educated soul. He beholds more things in heaven and upon earth than are dreamed of in any philosophy. When he has learned that he is not body with a mind which is ruled either from within or without, but that both can be made obedient servants to his real spiritual self, he has brought into expression that God-given dominion with which he was originally endowed.

"Spirit is the supreme essence of man's being. It is never diseased and never unhappy for, as that great soul, Emerson, says, 'It is the finite that suffers. The infinite lies stretched in smiling repose.' Job of your Bible told you that man was Spirit and the breath of the Almighty gave him life. It is indeed the Spirit in man which gives life and that Spirit rules his lower activities. Spirit issues commands with authority and all things become subordinate to righteous rule.

"A new era, wrapped in the garment of approaching day, is dawning in the hearts of men; and soon again will the virgin Spirit of God shine forth from the heart and the door again will open, by which all who will may find entrance to a larger and fuller life. Young, vibrant, with perennial youth and hope and endeavor, the soul of man stands on the threshold of a new era, more glorious than any other that has brightened the sky since Creation's dawn. The Star of Bethlehem shone brighter at Jesus' birth than it had before but soon its brightness will be like a noonday sun, for this new light foretells the day when the Christ is born in the hearts of all men."

CHAPTER VIII

THE next morning Chander Sen continued his talk. "I have been shown beyond a question of doubt that the human intelligence can be transmuted into Divine Intelligence. As this was made plain to me, I found that I could enter the Kingdom of God and that Kingdom was right within. Now I know that God is the only power, Omnipresent and Omniscient; and that sin, discord, sickness, old age, and death belong only to a past experience. I now perceive the reality and know that I had been lost in the mist of illusion. Time and space have completely disappeared and I know that I now dwell in the subjective and that it belongs to the objective world. Had it been possible for me to have held to the promptings and the glimpses the finer senses have revealed from time to time, how many weary and anxious hours would I have been saved. While in youth I, like the greater portion of humanity, decided that there was but one life to live and that was the gratification of self in every way, so I determined to get the most out of that life. I made self-seeking the principal aim in life and I gave the animal passions full sway, with the result that I dissipated the life fluids of my body until it was but the empty shell that you first saw. Let me bring forth a picture that will more graphically illustrate my thoughts."

He sat silent for a moment and a picture like those already described appeared upon one wall of the room. This was the picture of himself as we had seen him a short time ago. It was that of an old man, tottering along, leaning on his wooden staff. Following this was the likeness of the man as he appeared this morning. He continued, "The first represents the one who has dissipated the energies and life fluids of his body until nothing but the empty shell remains. The other represents the one who has conserved his energies and the vital life fluids within his body. You look upon this in my case as a complete and entire rejuvenation, which is true. But I look at it from another angle. How many could be as fortunate as I was, to have the help, sympathy, and assistance of those dear ones as I have had?

"In order that you may get my thought, let us follow the life of a person from birth to the end, as so many look upon death. The child is born. It is unconscious of the life-carrying fluids which course through its body, as they are inactive because the organs that generate life fluids are inactive and not yet developed. During this stage of development, if the child is normal, it is beautiful, active, and bubbling over with life. The life fluids are built up stronger and stronger, until the child reaches the stage of development where the life fluids are active, and they may be dissipated. If this dissipation takes place, in a few years the child begins to show age. The eyes lose their luster, the body its activity and grace. The features become set. In a few more years the brain loses its power of coordination with the muscles and the body is that of a decrepit old man or woman, but the empty shell of the former self.

"Then take the person who has conserved all the life fluids and allowed them to circulate in their natural course through the body, and see how strong and vigorous that one is. Should that one go on always conserving the life fluids, even though he did not perceive any higher idea of life than to be born, live a short time upon this earth, then pass on, the span of that life would be extended from three to

74

four times that of a person who has dissipated the life fluids. If he does perceive that there is a greater scheme in God's plan for him, he will at all times conserve the life fluids in the body, as he soon finds that they are a necessary adjunct for perfect development.

"It was only a short time ago that your learned men began to know of the delicate system of arteries and veins composing the circulatory system of your bodies. It is still left for them to determine that there is a far more delicate and subtle circulatory system throughout the body, which carries the life force to every atom. Through your nervous system this life force is sent to a set of cells in the brain. These cells, in turn, act as a distributor for the force and it is sent out to every atom of the body along the nerves, for which it has an affinity. It also acts as a protection for the nerves. If the life force is dissipated, the cells become set and cannot change for the new cells (that are formed to take their place) and the new cells are thrown off instead of the old ones, which gradually decompose and die. If the life force is conserved, the cells change as readily at five hundred years as at ten.

"It will be found that when all the life force is conserved, the body can be so charged with life that you can speak life into all forms. You can paint a picture, model a statue, or take any of your handiwork that expresses your ideal and breathe the breath of life into it and it will become alive. It will speak to you and to others who can see the life inspiration that you have spoken into it; and it will be active because you, the Lord God of you, has spoken and it is as He wills. But those forms will not assume the human, unless you carry them to the God Life. If you do give them life you must carry them through to the pure

75

God Life; then they are perfect forms, as you are perfect, and you have fulfilled your responsibility. This you will find is true genius.

"There is one vital error that I wish to point out. The genius, as you consider him, as he begins to develop, has consciously or unconsciously acquired the ability to conserve and send the life forces in their purity through their natural channels; this condition has animated his body and the creative faculty and he sees that there is something higher for him to express than the ordinary. While he conserves the life forces and gives them free rein, he will go on to more and more glorious achievements; but if he allows sex lust to creep in, he quickly loses his creative power. The body has been first built up by conserving the life forces until the cells are of a finer texture than the lower order of person who has dissipated the life force. By this time the genius has risen to fame and, not having developed his deeper perceptive or God power, is carried away by self-glory. He forsakes his guiding light because he has not been fully awakened; in the urge for greater excitement, he begins to dissipate the life forces and quickly loses all power. For if man does raise his thought above the animal passions and conserves the life forces until the body has begun to take on the finer texture, then allows himself to fall back, he will go back much more rapidly than one that has not been thus awakened.

"When one has been awakened so that he will conserve all the life forces and let them be distributed to the nerves in the natural way, then let them go coursing along the nerves to every atom of the body, without deforming it with thoughts of sex-lust or passion, the exhilaration will be permanent and the sensation will far transcend that of sex. The

76

serpent will be lifted up and will need to crawl on its belly through the murk and mire of lust and passion.

"If man could understand that this life fluid is many times more vital than a corresponding amount of pure blood, he would conserve instead of dissipate it. But he shuts his eyes to this fact (he may be entirely ignorant of it) and goes on, either in blindness or ignorance, until the Reaper arrives. Then a wail goes up, for he does not admire the harvest.

"You look upon old age with veneration and snow-white locks as a crown of honor, which I would not detract from in any way. But as you look upon the picture, I leave it for you to decide which is the more to be honored, he with the snow-white locks, who has by ignorance or direct perversity brought decrepitude upon himself or the one who, in maturity, becomes more vital, strong, and better equipped to meet the advancing years and because of them is more kind and generous. I recognize that the one who reaches the end through ignorance is to be pitied, while the one who knows and reaches the same end, is unspeakable."

CHAPTER IX

FROM this time on we applied ourselves diligently to learn our alphabet with Chander Sen as our instructor. The days passed altogether too quickly and April was drawing to a close with the greater part of the records still to be translated; but we were consoling ourselves that we would be able to return and finish the translations. Although our friends had translated a large portion of these records for us, they had insisted upon our study of the characters so that we would be able to translate them for ourselves.

During the preceding September we had arranged to meet a party in the Gobi Desert and they were to accompany us to the site of three of the ancient ruined cities, the locations of which are given by some of these records. While we had not, as yet, seen these records, we had been told of their existence. Those which we had previously seen and which had aroused our curiosity were but copies of the records we had before us. Both of the sets place the dates of these cities back two hundred thousand years. It is claimed that the inhabitants were in a high state of civilization, as they knew the arts and crafts and were able to work with the metals; that gold was a very common metal, so common that they used it in making drinking vessels and for shoeing their horses. It is claimed that these people had a good command over all the natural forces as well as their own God-given powers. In fact, the legends—if legends they are—as told therein are quite similar to those of Greek mythology. If the maps are correct, this huge empire covered the greater portion of Asia and extended into Europe as far as the Mediterranean Sea, where France is now located, and the greatest elevation was about six hundred feet above sea level. It is claimed that this was a great plain area, very productive and well populated and a colony of the Motherland. There is no question that, if the remains of these cities can be found and uncovered, some very valuable history will be disclosed, as the description the records gave of this country far outshone that of ancient Egypt for pomp and splendor during the dynasties of its seven kings. Even before the reign of these kings, it is described as being far more prosperous. The people ruled themselves; there were no wars and no vassals or slaves. They unquestionably named their ruler, "Directive Principle," and they loved and obeyed that Directive Principle. These records state that the first king of the first dynasty usurped the rule from the Directive Principle and set himself upon a throne as ruler.

Time had passed rapidly. We were busy getting everything in readiness to join the expedition, as we were obliged to be on our way in order to keep our appointment in May at the meeting place agreed upon, where we were to replenish our supplies and equip the main expedition for the final journey.

Words absolutely fail me when I undertake to record my thoughts and feelings as the time for our departure drew near. Every hour of our stay had been a joy, not one being dull.

Although we had been with these people and shared their homes for more than five months, the time had passed so rapidly that it seemed but a few days. Yet a world of possibilities had been opened to us. It was as though the door had been thrown wide open. Everyone felt the boundless possibilities — and still we hesitated to step through the door, just as we hesitated to leave these magnificent people whom we looked upon as brothers.

I believe there is a time in the life of every mortal when he or she can see the door fully opened — just as each of us saw it that beautiful April morning — and each and every one can see the vast possibilities that may be attained. (I am going to ask the readers to throw aside all prejudices for a time and, if they are able to do so, see as we saw. I do not expect you to believe but I do want you to understand that it is one thing to write about these people and an entirely different thing just to sit at their feet and listen.) It seemed that if we would walk boldly up and step through the door, all attainment would be ours — yet we hesitated. Why was it so? Because we did not fully believe; we allowed tradition to drag us back and close the door; then we said the hand of fate had closed it to us. But we must come to realize there is no fate save that which we ourselves allow.

Here were a kindly, simple, yet most magnificent people, some of whom for generations and perhaps always have lived just through that door and that life is practical to them. There is no precedent nor tradition here, nothing but a pure, honest life, well lived and lived right here on this earth. I leave it to the reader to make the contrast.

We did hesitate to leave these dear kindly souls to whom we had become so attached in the last few months, yet we knew that other things awaited us and we looked forward eagerly to them. We bade our friends good-by that beautiful April morning, with cordial handshakes and salutations, amid hearty invitations to come again. With a final good-by and Godspeed, our faces were turned northward, this time actually to cross the great Gobi, with its tales of terrible hardships as dim visions in our imaginations; but we were unafraid, for Emil and Jast were again with us, and Chander Sen in Neprow's place.

To us, who had visited many lands, as the company swung along the trail it was but a part of the day's work. Everyone in our little band was glad to be there. Not one but recognized that a new world had begun to open and unfold. All recognized the remoteness of the country and the hazards of an ordinary trip of this nature, yet there was that irresistible urge to go on. With the absolute confidence we had in our great friends, all fear or thought of inconvenience for self was thrown to the winds and we entered into the zest of the thing with the enthusiasm of schoolboys.

We were accustomed to the remote places of the earth, but never had we experienced a country so remote yet one where we could travel with the freedom and ease that we were experiencing here. Do you wonder that we were infatuated with the country and our benefactors? We felt that we could go right on north until we had negotiated the polar regions and conquered them. We had not gone far when one of our party remarked, "If we could travel as those fellows can, this part would be easy. Just because we cannot travel as they do, they plod along with us."

All went well until the evening of the seventh day out. At about five o'clock that afternoon we were just emerging from a deep ravine which we had followed down in order to gain access to the more open country below, when one of the party called out that there were horsemen in the distance. We turned our glasses upon them and counted twenty-seven horsemen who seemed to be fully armed. We reported this to Jast and he said they probably were one of the roving bands that infest the country. We asked if they were one of the bandit bands and he said that he suspected they were, as they did not appear to be tending any flocks.

We left the trail and proceeded to a clump of trees and made camp for the night. While the camp was being prepared, two of our party crossed the stream near which we were camping and climbed to the top of a ridge that would give them an outlook over the rolling country. When they had gained the summit they stopped and, placing their field glasses to their eyes, stood for a moment, then turned and hurried toward camp. As soon as they came within hailing distance they reported that the party of horsemen was not over three miles away and was riding toward our camp. At this time someone remarked that he believed it was going to storm. We looked and, sure enough, there was a heavy bank of clouds gathering in the northwest and fog was drifting in from every direction. We became very uneasy as we could now see the band of horsemen through the approaching storm, coming down a rolling slope directly toward our camp. We were very much disturbed about the appearance of this band. Although there were thirty-two in our party, we did not have a firearm of any description.

At that moment the storm broke upon us with all the fury of a blizzard. For a few moments the wind lashed and roared and drove the fine particles of snow around us with the fury of a seventy-mile gale and it looked as if we would be obliged to move our camp to escape the falling limbs that were being broken from the trees by the storm. Then everything became calm where we were, and we thought for a moment that it had been only a squall, such as often happens in that country, and that it would soon blow over.

Since there was a dim half light which enabled us

to see, we turned to and set the camp in order. We were occupied with this work for about half an hour and had not given a thought to either the storm or the supposed bandits who had caused so much uneasiness a short time before. As we stopped a moment for breath, our Chief walked to the entrance of the tent and looked out, then turned and said, "The storm seems to be raging a short distance away, but where we are there is scarcely a breath of air stirring. Just look, the tents and trees around are hardly moving and the air seems warm and balmy." A number of our party followed him outside and we stood for a moment wondering. While we had been in the tent and occupied, we had been half conscious of the noise the storm was making but we supposed it had blown over and was traveling up the ravine, as some of the storms in that country come on like a cyclone and travel for miles before they expend their fury and after they have passed there is a dead calm. This was not the case here. The blizzard was raging with all its fury within a hundred feet of us but where we stood the air was still and warm. Our former experience had been that the cold was intense and pierced one through and through, while the wind drove the icy needle-like particles of snow around and along with it in blinding fury until one was nearly suffocated.

Suddenly the circle lighted up as if by magic. As we stood wondering, we thought we heard shouts of men above the din of the storm. Supper was announced; we went in and sat down. While we were eating, one of the party wondered what had become of the horsemen we had seen descending the slope. Another said, "We thought we had heard shouts while we were outside and wondered if we could not be of some assistance in case they were lost in the blizzard." Jast stated that these men belonged to one of the most notorious bands of bandits which roamed the nearby country. He added that they did nothing but rob and plunder villages and drive off the herds of sheep and goats. After supper, during a lull in the storm, we could hear shouting and the lunging and snorting of horses, sounding as though they would break from control. Although they seemed but a short distance away, we could not see them, so dark and dense was the snow that was whirled along by the wind; neither could we see any sign of a camp fire.

In a few moments Emil arose and said he would invite them to our camp. Unless they were well prepared, it would be impossible for man or beast to survive the storm until morning, as the cold was growing intense outside. As he was preparing to leave the tent, two of our party asked to be permitted to accompany him. Emil seemed pleased; he accepted and they disappeared in the storm. After about twenty minutes had elapsed they reappeared, followed by twenty of the bandit band leading their horses. They told us afterwards that seven had become separated from them and were probably lost in the storm. Those who gathered in our circle were a unique and motley lot of half-wild looking creatures. The moment they entered the circle of light they became suspicious that there was some plot to capture them. They showed their alarm until Emil assured them they were at liberty to go any time they wished and showed them that we had no mode of defense if they wished to attack us. This, their leader said, they had prepared to do when they saw us emerge from the ravine before the storm came on. After the storm came, they had become bewildered and lost their way so they did not know where their camp was located. When Emil and the two from our party had found them they were huddled together against a cliff about a hundred yards downstream. The leader said if they were driven out they would certainly perish. Emil assured them that this would not happen.

They made their horses secure for the night among the trees, then gathered in a group by themselves, sat down, and began eating dried goat meat and yak butter which they had taken from their saddle pouches. While they were thus occupied, they kept their arms near at hand and would start and listen at any increased sound. They talked and gesticulated freely. Jast told us they were wondering at our equipment and the light; why the wind was not blowing, why it was warm within the circle, and why the horses were so content. One of the party, who was doing most of the talking, had heard of our friends before. He was telling the group that these people were like gods and could destroy them (the bandits) in an instant if they would. Jast also said that some of the party were attempting to influence the others to take everything we had and go on, as they thought it was a plot to capture them; but that this one man was standing firm that we should not be molested. He was telling them that if they did harm us they would all be destroyed. After the talk had gone on for considerable time, eight of them arose and came over to us and told Jast they would not stay; that they were very much afraid and were going to try and go to their camp, as it was located on the same stream but a few miles below. They had been able to get their location from the clump of trees where we were encamped. They then mounted their horses and rode away downstream.

In about twenty minutes they all returned, saying the snow had fallen so deep their horses could not travel and face the storm, which was the heaviest they had experienced for many years. Then they began making themselves comfortable for the night.

One of our party said, "Well, I suppose they will be more comfortable here, even if they are afraid, than they would be out in the storm." Jast turned to us and said, "The Father's house is where you are abiding; if you are within that house and do there abide, you are in the glad spirit of the Father. Of what avail is the warmth and cheer that abides within the house if you are not of the house, or know not the warmth and cheer that abides therein? You may invite those that remain just without and they will not enter, for they know not where you abide. These dear ones here, while they feel the warmth, will not come nearer for the reason that they have always preyed upon their fellow men and they cannot understand that those same men whom they have looked upon as legitimate prey should befriend them without some reason for doing so, especially as they do not belong to their band. They do not know that within the snow or cold, or heaviest storm, the Father abides; and that those who make His home their home and therein abide cannot be harmed by storm or wind or tide. It is only when you are out of contact with God that the winds, the storms, and tides sweep over you.

"It is when one can stand steadfastly and unwaveringly with his eyes fixed directly on God, knowing and seeing no other, that he can accomplish what you now see. Our thought is, 'I stand steadfastly with my eyes fixed on You, O Father; knowing naught but You, Father; and I see naught but God in all things. I stand firmly on the Holy Mount, knowing naught but Your Love, Life, and Wisdom. Your Divine Spirit pervades me always. It surrounds me and abounds within and without me always. I know,

Father, that this is not for me alone, but it is for all Thy children. I know, Father, that I have naught but that which they have and there is naught but God for all. I thank Thee, Father.'

"The real peace may be found even in the heart of the storm; but deep in the heart of the man who has found himself, is the true calm. On the contrary, man may be in the remote wilderness alone with the twilight and the vast silence of nature and yet be torn by the winds of passion or shaken by the thunders of fear.

"Nature, carelessly observed, seems to have given brute strength, greed, and capacity for shedding weaker animals' blood an incomparable advantage; but notice the following simple facts that few have thought about.

"There are more lambs in the world than lions. That is not an accident. Nature is not a blind, blundering thing. Nature is God at work and God neither wastes material nor does He blunder in His building. Does it not strike you as a strange thing that in the melting pot of Nature's primal forces the lion had not eaten up the lamb before man appeared upon the scene? The lamb has literally whipped the lion in the struggle for existence. Nor is it man's siding with the lamb against the lion that explains the result. In all probability man began his career of slaughter by killing the docile first. It is certain that he kills more lambs than lions. It is not man but Nature that pronounces condemnation of lion's kin. Reflect a moment and you will see that Nature cannot give distinctive strength in opposite directions to the same animal. The lion is a great fighter but a slow breeder. All the strength of his fine body goes to fighting form. Having young is detrimental and becomes the incident of his life. The lamb, on the other hand, is not a fighter and therefore is weak. The lamb spends no energy in fighting and accordingly is a better breeder. Nature acknowledges that in creating the lion she made a mistake. She is correcting that mistake. The lion and all other animals whose instinct is to kill are disappearing.

"There are no exceptions to this sentence of extinction pronounced by Nature's immutable law against all beings of the preying kind. Nature rules according to an eternal equity and, by the very law of the universe, the fighter fights a losing battle, always has and always will, whether he be the animal or the animal man, in the forest or in the city, now and forever. The lion loses. He loses when he wins. He dies when he kills. He is by the very nature of things eating his own kind when he rends the warm flesh of the lamb he tore from the flock. When the first lion struck his prey with his mighty paw and growled through his bloody chops the delight he felt, he was singing, not the death of the helpless that he was eating, but the funeral hymn of his own kind. Savagery is a poor rallying point. Lions do not herd. Bears do not go in flocks. Savages among men form small groups and fight each other. Wildness turns on its own kind among beasts or men and is a source of weakness.

"In the analogy of things wild beasts must go. No great soldier ever really conquered anything. His victories are all illusions. Soldiers' empires, if they rest on nothing more substantial than the sword, swiftly fall to pieces. In the end, the soldiers must repudiate force and resort to justice and reason or their empires crumble. The beast of prey, whether he is brute or human, is solitary, hopeless, and helpless, irrevocably doomed, for gentleness is the real strength. Gentleness is the lion, with all of the lion's attributes, except the taste for blood and slowly all life is coming beneath its all-conquering rule.

"Man is made or unmade by himself. In the armory of thought he forges the weapons by which he destroys himself. He also fashions the tools with which he builds for himself heavenly mansions of joy, strength, and peace. By the right choice and true application of thought, man ascends to the Divine Perfection. By the abuse and wrong application of thought, he descends below the level of the beast. Between these two extremes are all of the grades of character and man is their maker and master.

"These bandits are the remnants of a once great and prosperous people. Their forefathers inhabited this country when it was a beautiful, thriving, industrial empire. They knew the sciences and arts. They also knew their own origin and power and they worshipped that origin and power only. There came a time when they began to look to the body for pleasure and in time the body failed them. Then a great cataclysm swept over the land, devastating it and leaving only a few scattered people on the higher ground. These developed into communities and became the larger races of Europe.

"The region where we are and that of the Gobi were cut off and raised bodily until nothing grew. The people were so nearly destroyed that there were only a few isolated communities and, at times, only one or two families left. These gathered in bands and are the ancestors of the present people. They cannot prosper, as they are continually at war with each other. While their history and origin have been forgotten, their religion and legends can be traced to the one source. Wherever you find them you will find some of the fundamentals alike, although their forms differ widely."

Here Jast said that he feared he had already wearied us, as all our friends were fast asleep. We looked in the direction of the bandits and, sure enough, they were all asleep. They, as well as we, had forgotten the storm, which was still unabated. We went into the tent and retired, again thankful to our great friends.

When we awoke the next morning, the sun was shining and the whole camp was astir. We dressed hastily and went out to find that the company, bandits and all, were waiting for us. At breakfast we were told that it had been arranged we should travel as far as the bandits' camp together, as it would be easier to break trail when we were all together. The bandits seemed pleased at the prospect but I can not say we were, for we were told that there were about one hundred and fifty at their camp. By the time we had finished breakfast all vestige of the storm had passed; so we broke camp and started out with the bandits and their horses to break trail, leaving the others to follow with the camp equipment.

Although the bandits' camp was not over twelve miles down the river, we did not reach there until after midday, when we were only too pleased to stop for a little rest. We found the camp very comfortable, with ample room to accommodate all our party. After lunch it was decided that we could make better headway if we waited a day or two to allow the new snow that had fallen to settle, as we would be obliged to cross a divide of about fourteen thousand feet elevation the next day. The weather did not prove to be as warm as was expected, so our stay was prolonged for four days. The whole village treated us with the greatest respect and did everything in their power to make our stay comfortable.

When we were leaving, two of the men asked if they could join our party. As we were expecting to recruit a number of helpers in the next large village, about seventy miles farther on, we gladly accepted them and they were with us until we returned that fall.

When we left the village, nearly one-half of the population accompanied us to the summit of the high divide in order to assist in breaking trail through the deep snow, and we were very thankful for their kindly efforts, as it proved a very difficult ascent. At the summit we bade farewell to our bandit friends and went on to the appointed meeting place, arriving there May 28, three days after the arrival of the friends we had made the appointment with the fall before.

CHAPTER X

AFTER resting for a week and reassembling our outfit, the combined expedition set out for the ancient city of the Uigurs, where we arrived June 30. Here we set to work immediately and when the first pit was down to a depth of fifty feet we encountered the walls of an ancient building. When we had proceeded to a depth of a little more than ninety feet, we broke into a large room where there were a number of gold, silver, bronze, and clay statues, all beautifully wrought. After the work had progressed far enough to prove beyond a question of doubt that this had once been a very large city, we went on to the second location. Here we went down about forty feet before we came upon anything that could be called definite proof of a former civilization. Again we did enough work to prove that we were in the ruins of a large ancient city.

We removed to a third location, where we expected to find evidence that would prove this the oldest and largest of the three cities.

In order to conserve time and resources we had organized our forces into four parties. Three of these parties were made up of a leader and six assistants. This gave seven men to each party. To this combined force was assigned all the excavation work and its management, each party being assigned eight hours out of the twenty-four. The fourth party, consisting of the remainder of the personnel of the expedition, was assigned the duties of the camp. I was in the party of which our Chief was the leader. We were assigned the eight hours from midnight until eight in the morning.

After we had completed the discovery of the first pit and had gained access to four of the underground chambers or rooms, we cleared away enough of the debris to show beyond a question of doubt that this was the oldest and largest city of the three and that it was rich in treasure.

One morning the party which relieved our Chief's party reported that there were horsemen approaching our camp from the north. When we reached the surface we found they were headed in our direction and it looked as though they were another bandit band, since they were evidently following the trail we had made on our way there. As we stood looking, Jast came up and said, "They are a party of bandits who are determined to loot the camp but I do not think we need fear." We waited for them to approach and they came on to within five hundred yards of our camp, then halted.

After a short interval two of the men rode up and, after exchanging greetings, asked what we were doing there. They were told we were attempting to find a ruined city. To this they replied they did not believe a word of what we said. They suspected we were looking for gold and they had come to take our equipment and supplies from us. We asked if they were government soldiers, to which they replied they did not recognize any government, as the strongest party was the one that won in that country. As they saw no evidence of firearms, I believe they came to the conclusion that there must be a larger force than was evidenced by what they could see. They returned to their band to talk over the situation.

After a time the two came back and told us that if we submitted peacefully they would not harm any of us but if we did not they would advance and shoot everyone who showed resistance. We were given ten minutes to decide and after that time they would

93

advance without further preliminaries. To this Jast replied that we would neither resist nor surrender. This seemed to anger them and, wheeling their horses, they started back toward the band, waving their arms. Then the whole band came toward us at full gallop. I confess that I was badly frightened but almost instantly we seemed to be surrounded by a number of shadowy forms on horseback, galloping around us. Then these forms became more lifelike and increased in numbers. Evidently our visitors had seen what we were witnessing, for their horses were either reined in quickly or stopped of their own accord as they began to rear and plunge and get beyond control of their riders. In a moment there was wild confusion among the band, which numbered about seventy-five horsemen. The horses began plunging right and left, beyond all control of the riders and this ended in a wild retreat, with our phantom horsemen, as we called them, in close pursuit.

After the excitement was over, our Chief and two of the party, including myself, walked out to where the main band had halted and could find no tracks except those made by the robbers themselves. We were very much mystified at this since the relief had looked as real to us as did the bandits and the rescuers had seemed to have come from all sides. We fully expected to find the tracks of their horses in the sand, as well as the tracks of the horses the bandits were riding.

When we returned, Jast said, "The phantom horsemen, as you call them, were only pictures, made so real that you, as well as the bandits, could see them. In a word they were the pictures of other occurrences that we were able to produce in so lifelike a manner that they could not be distinguished from the real occurrence. We are able to produce them for our own protection as well as for that of others and no one has been harmed. Where a definite purpose is served, there is no harm in the outcome. A doubt had arisen in the minds of the bandits. It was not logical that an expedition like this would venture so far away without some protection and we were able to take advantage of this to frighten them. They are very superstitious and always on the lookout for trickery. That type is the most susceptible to fear and they saw just what they expected to find. If we had not used this method, we should in all probability have been obliged to destroy a number of the band before they would have left us in peace. As it is we shall hear no more of them." We were not molested again.

After we had accomplished sufficient work to convince us that these three cities existed, it was suggested that we should fill all the pits, in order to protect them from any roving band that might discover the work, as such a discovery would lead to wholesale plundering for the treasure alone. There are legends among nearly all these bands that these great cities exist and that they contain hoards of gold. As we finished work, each pit was filled, so as to leave as little trace as possible; and the first storm would remove any trace which we had left. The sand is continually shifting in this country and this alone makes it very difficult to locate any of these ruins. It would have been impossible for us to discover any of the locations without the assistance of our friends. We were told that similar ruins extend well into Southern Siberia.

There is unmistakable evidence that a vast population had flourished here and that they had reached a high state of civilization. There is also unlimited proof that these people understood agriculture, mining, textiles and their allied industries, reading,

95

writing, and all the sciences. It is very evident that the history of these people is the history of the Aryan race.

While seated at the table the afternoon of our last day, one of the party asked Emil whether the history of this great race could be traced and written. He answered that it could, that the city beneath the site of our camp contained the absolute proof in written records, which, when found and translated, would give a concurrent and direct history of this people.

Here the conversation was interrupted by a man appearing at the door of the tent and asking if he could come in. Emil, Jast, and Chander Sen arose and hurried to the entrance to meet him. By the greetings extended we saw they were very well acquainted and our Chief arose and joined them. At the door of the tent we saw him stop and stare for a moment; then he walked quickly out of the door with both hands extended, saying, "Well, well, this is indeed a surprise." A medley of voices arose, as both men and women began to exchange greetings with him and the three that had stepped through the door after him. At this, all seated at the table arose and crowded outside, where we found a group of fourteen newcomers. The party included Emil's mother, our hostess from the village of our former winter quarters, the beautiful lady who had presided at the banquet that we attended in Emil's home, and Emil's son and daughter. In all they were a merry crowd and it brought back remembrances of gatherings of former days.

The surprise was complete and we showed it, but the most complete surprise was shown by the friends who had joined us on this expedition. As we looked at them, we knew that their curiosity was getting beyond all bounds. They had not seen these appearances and disappearances as we had and during the

press of the expedition work we had been so engrossed that we had neglected to tell them of anything
but fragmentary incidents. Coming, as this had, vir-
tually from a clear sky, it left them absolutely non-
plussed. Of course we were heartily enjoying this at
their expense.

After introductions and greetings had been
extended all around, the man who had charge of the
camp and equipment sought Emil and our Chief.
With every evidence of abject helplessness, he said,
"How am I going to feed all these people? Our
supplies have not yet arrived and we have barely
enough provisions left for ourselves for this and the
morning meal, since we have made every arrangement to start on our return trip." While they were
conversing they had drawn together and the leader
of the combined expedition had overheard a part of
the conversation. He stepped over and joined them.
As he did so, I could hear him ask, "Where in the
name of heaven did all these people come from?"
Our Chief looked at him with a smile and said, "You
have just hit it, Ray, they did come direct from heav-
en. See, there are no conveyances." Ray answered,
"But the thing that puzzles me most is, they don't
seem to have any wings. As they do not have wings,
we should have heard the thud when they landed in
the sand, especially as there are so many of them;
but we did not even hear that. So we are going to
decide for the time that your suggestion is right and
perfectly logical."

Emil then turned to the company and said he
would be obliged, in order to allay the fears of the
steward, to admonish the visitors for not bringing
along their provisions. At this the steward seemed
greatly embarrassed and said he did not think of
putting it quite so bluntly but, nevertheless, the fact
still remained that there certainly were not enough

edibles to go around. Here the visitors joined in a merry laugh, which seemed to embarrass him still more. Then Emil's mother said there was no need for embarrassment or inconvenience. Our hostess and the beautiful lady joined in saying they would gladly take charge and be responsible for the supper, as they fully expected to share the meal with us. This relieved the steward and he quickly accepted the proffered service.

The afternoon was now well advanced. It was one of those days in the Gobi when the weather fairly fawns upon the earth for one moment, then in the next instant may transform the scene into an inferno of relentless fury. Every available canvas was secured and spread upon the sand, just outside the circle of the camp. To an outsider, the scene would have had the appearance of a merry picnic party, which indeed it was. When the canvas was all spread, the containers, which were used both for cooking and serving the camp meals, were brought out with their contents and placed on the canvas. Then the whole company gathered around.

We could still see evidences of wonder and perplexity on the faces of those who had lately joined the party. Ray, the leader, looked at the containers and said that if he saw rightly the amount of food the containers held and if that amount could be stretched sufficiently to feed that hungry mob, he was going to keep his eyes open for the performance of a miracle. One of our party said, "You better keep your eyes wide open, for that is just what you are going to see." Our Chief said, "That is twice you have guessed right today, Ray." At this the three ladies began serving from the containers. As each plate was served, it was passed on and an empty plate was received for the full one until all had been served most generously.

As the serving progressed, we could see that Ray was getting more restless; and when his plate came to him he passed it on, remarking that he could get along with a much less liberal helping. Our hostess assured him that he need not fear, as there would be a plentiful supply for all.

After all had been served bountifully, he again looked at the containers. When he saw that the contents had not been diminished, he arose and said, "At the risk of being impolite, ill-mannered, and a bounder, I am going to ask if I may sit by you three ladies, as I fully acknowledge my curiosity has so deliberately taken the upper hand that I cannot eat a bite." The ladies said they would look upon it as an act of courtesy if he wished to sit by them. Whereupon he walked over and sat down on the edge of the canvas, between Emil's mother and the beautiful lady.

When he was seated, someone asked for bread. There was but one piece remaining on the box lid that served in place of a tray. The beautiful lady held out her hands and almost instantly there was a large loaf of bread in them. This she passed to our hostess, who began cutting it, preparatory to serving. At this the leader arose and asked if they would kindly permit him to see the loaf as it was. The loaf was passed to him and, after examining it critically for a moment, he passed it back. We could see that he was very much agitated. He walked away a few steps, then returned and, addressing himself directly to the lady, said, "I do not wish to seem impertinent but this has muddled my thoughts to such an extent that I cannot refrain from asking questions." She bowed and said he was at liberty to ask any questions he wished. He said, "Do you mean to tell me that you are able to set aside all the known natural laws — at least those that we know of—without the least exertion and bring forth bread from an unseen or invisible supply?" The lady replied, "To us the supply is not unseen; it is always visible." Then it was perceived that as our hostess cut and served the loaf it did not diminish.

He became more calm, again took his place, and the lady continued: "If you could only see that the tragedy of Jesus' life ended with the crucifixion, that the joy of the Christ life began with the resurrection, and that the goal of every life should be the resurrection rather than the crucifixion. In this way all may follow him into the more abundant life of the Christ in them. Can you think of a more joyous and abundant life than to be one with this Mighty Power, this power of the Christ within? It is here you may know that you were created to have dominion over every form, thought, word, or condition. In living this life, which is the fulfillment of every need, you will find that you are living an exact, scientific life.

"Jesus increased the few loaves and fishes the little lad had, until he was able to supply ample for the multitude. You will observe that he bade them sit down in an orderly expectant attitude, ready to receive the increased supply by fulfilling the law. If you are to find joy and satisfaction in the life of Jesus, you must fulfill the law of his life by acting in harmony with his ideals. You cannot stand and worry as to how you are to be fed. If Jesus had allowed this, the multitude never would have been satisfied. Instead, He quietly blessed and gave thanks for that which he had and the supply was increased in sufficient measure to meet every need.

"Living did not become a difficult problem until man disobeyed and refused to listen to the Inner Voice. When he returns and again learns to listen to that Inner Voice he will cease to labor for the means of a living, but he will work for the joy of creating. He will enter into the joy of creating and he will create under the law of the Lord or Word of God. Through His Word he will find that he can move upon the all-loving and all-enfolding substance of God and bring into visibility every ideal he holds in thought. It was in this way, step by step, that Jesus mounted to the heights and proved the supremacy of the Christ in Him over the limited concept of mortal thought. When this is realized, work becomes a joyous quality of one's being. Jesus proved that the truly spiritual life is the only joyous life. He became clothed with dignity and glory because of his victory; yet that victory left him as free as a little child. Although the world is not wholly awake to its desire, it is this desire of joy and great blessing that it is seeking. Man may seek satisfaction in the pursuit of personal things, unmindful of the law that says he shall lose that which he seeks for selfish gain. But through the losing he soon finds that the fall of the personal but marks the ascent of the spiritual. He realizes that *man's extremity is God's opportunity.*

"You must know that you are entitled to every good and perfect gift of God, and you must prepare to receive those gifts through the knowledge of God as your Divine nature. *If you separate yourself from God in thought, you will also separate yourself from him in manifestation.* In order to enter fully into the joy of life, you must seek life and joy, for the fullness and joy that that life gives to all humanity.

"The laws for the establishment of heaven here on earth, which Jesus taught and which you have seen applied in a very small measure, are exact and scientific. Man, being the son and true likeness of God, contains within himself the true spirit of God, his Father. He can discern and use the laws of his creative parent and bring them into full operation in his world of affairs, if he only will." Then she said they would be pleased to answer any questions he might like to ask.

Ray said he did not have any questions to ask, for he had been too deeply stirred to want to ask questions. He just wanted to think. He said he had some things he wanted to say and he hoped they would not take offense, for offense was not intended in any way. He continued. "We came here, as we supposed, to find the remains of a people long since dead and gone. Instead, we find a people living a far more wonderful and active life than can be comprehended. If this thing that we have seen could be heralded abroad, you would have the whole world bowing at your feet." The three ladies said they did not wish the world to bow at their feet but they longed to see all mankind bowing at God's feet. They went on to say that mankind already had too many idols. The ideal was the thing really needed.

Here the visitors, with the exception of the one who had called at the door of the tent, arose, saying they must be on their way. With hearty handshakes and Godspeed and invitations to visit them at any time, they disappeared as suddenly as they had come, leaving Ray and his party staring at the place where they had stood. After a moment he turned to the man who had remained and asked his name. He was told that it was Bagget Irand.

Then Ray said to him, "Do you mean to say that you are able to come and go at will, without any visible means of conveyance, as we have just seen, defying every known law of gravity or physics?"

Bagget Irand answered, "We do not defy any law, neither do we harm a single law of man or God. We cooperate with and work according to all laws, both of Nature and God. The means of locomotion which we use, although invisible to you, are perfectly visible to us. The trouble is you do not see them; consequently you do not believe. We see, believe, and know and we are able to utilize them. When you open your understanding to know and see and use them, you will soon find that the law which we use is definite and far more capable of being put to greater uses for mankind than the limited laws which you see and use. Some day you will find that you have only touched the surface of man's possibilities. We are always pleased to assist you in any way we can."

Chander Sen said that this friend had come to invite us to return to our outfitting point by way of his village, as the trail was shorter and the distance could be made with one day less travel at this time of the year. This invitation was readily accepted and Bagget Irand said he would return with us. It developed later that he was a descendant of the once prosperous people that had inhabited the Gobi region.

CHAPTER XI

WE HAD finished the work mapped out for the combined expedition and were prepared for an early morning start for our base, where the company would separate and all except a party of eleven would return to their respective homes. Four of the party, myself included, had decided to accept the invitation of our friends to return to the village of the Temple of the Tau Cross, our former winter quarters.

As we stood watching the sunset, on the eve of our departure, one of the party said that he had begun to wonder how old civilization and religion really were and whether the two had really come hand-in-hand down the long ages of time. Jast replied, "That depends upon what you mean by religion. If by the use of the word, 'religion' you mean creed, dogma or sect, or perhaps superstition, it is very young and does not antedate twenty thousand years. But, if by the word you mean a reverence for the true philosophy of life, a true reverence for life itself, thus a true reverence for the sublime purity of God, of the great Creative Cause, then you may trace this back beyond all history, all mythology, all allegory, to the time of man's first advent upon earth. Before kings, emperors, or man-made rule held sway in the heart of the first man there burned or shone forth the greatest reverence for the source of all life and the beauty of that life; the beauty and reverence of that pure soul shines undimmed through the long ages and so it will shine on undimmed through all eternity.

"When man first took up life, he knew full well the source. He had the deepest reverence for that source and that reverence you now know as the Christ. But, as we come on down the dim corridors of time, we find them divided into the innumerable sects, creeds, and dogmas until those corridors are divided into such a network that they present a veil of disbelief and superstition. Who, I ask, divided them — did God or man? Who is responsible for the great vortex of sin and inharmony this division has caused? Will you pause for a moment and think deeply, then ask yourselves, is it God or man that is responsible? Then think, does God sit somewhere in the sky looking down on this great web, altering a condition here or a condition there, interfering here or smoothing out a life there, praising one or condemning another, holding up the hands of one while he tramples the other? No, if there be a true giver of life, he must be Omnipotent, Omnipresent, Omniscient, far above, around, and in all, pouring out his life to all, through all and above all, else he is not a true giver of all life. Thus you may differentiate this idea into the innumerable varieties of form but, when you reach the final one, you will find that you reach the one at the beginning also; and the two become a cycle with no beginning and no end. Were this not so, there could be no basis, no hypothesis, no truth."

Here someone asked, "Do you attempt to overcome death?" The answer was, "Oh, no, we rise up over death by letting life express to its absolute fullness. Thus, we do not know even what death is. To us there is nothing but more abundant life. The great error of the majority is that they attempt to hide their religion behind some veil or secret instead of throwing it open to the broad expanse of God's pure sunlight."

Someone of the party asked whether Jesus abode with them, meaning Jast's people. He replied, "No, Jesus does not live with us. He is only drawn to us by

105

the thoughts we have in common, the same as he is drawn to all by the thoughts they have in common. Jesus abides only to be of service, as all great souls do."

He went on to say, "It was while sojourning in northern Arabia that Jesus had access to the library that had been collected from India, Persia, and the Trans-Himalayan region. Here Jesus first contacted the secret teachings of the Brotherhood. These teachings only served to drive home more firmly the conviction already forming, that the true mystery of life was God expressed through the Christ in the individual. He saw that, in order to express this fully, he must withdraw from all forms of worship and worship God expressing through the individual, and God alone. He saw that, in order to demonstrate this fully, he would be obliged to withdraw from those who had taught him, even though by withdrawing he should incur their displeasure. This did not deter him for a moment, so steadfast was he in his devotion to his cause and the great service he saw he could render to the world by that devotion.

"He saw that if man ever arose to the lofty power of that mighty Indwelling Presence; if a mighty Son of God, one in whom the Divine Wisdom abode in fullest measure; one rich in the outpouring richness of all of God's treasures, the fountain of the outpouring waters of life, the Lord, or law of compassion and wisdom; was actually to take flesh upon earth, he must come forth and claim these possessions. Then, with pure motive he must live the life and he would bring forth that life, to which manifest Presence the name of the Christ has been given.

"He stood forth and boldly proclaimed that the Christ that abode in him abode in all; that the celestial voice that proclaimed him the Beloved Son proclaimed all sons of God, joint heirs, and brothers all. This epoch is marked at his baptism when the Spirit was seen descending from heaven like a dove upon him and it abode with him. He also said all are God's, manifest in the flesh.

"He boldly taught that ignorance is the cause of all sin. He saw that, in order to practice forgiveness or the science of forgiving, man must be enlightened to the fact that man has the power to forgive all sin, discord, and inharmony; that it is not God who forgives sin, for God has nothing to do with the sin, sickness, and inharmony of man; that man, himself, brought these into being and man is the only one who can erase or forgive them. He saw that man must learn that ignorance is disregard and lack of understanding both of Divine Mind as the Creative Principle and of his relation to that Principle. He saw that man may have all intellectual knowledge and be versed in worldly affairs, yet if he does not recognize the Christ as the living, vitalizing essence of God within him, he is grossly ignorant of the most important factor governing his life. He quickly saw the inconsistency of asking a perfectly just and loving Father to heal a disease or sin. He taught that disease is the effect of sin and that forgiveness is an important factor in healing; that sickness is not punishment sent from God, as many believe it to be, but is the result of man's misunderstanding of his real being. He taught that it is the Truth which sets free. The purity of his teachings has caused them to outlive those of his teachers.

"When Peter said that he forgave seven times, Jesus' answer was that he forgave seventy times seven, then went on forgiving until the act was universal. In order to forgive hate, he centered his attention on love. This was not only when it touched his life, but when he saw it manifest in the world about him. This Truth was the inherent light that he saw in all, which would lead them out of darkness when applied with understanding. He knew that every overcomer was covenanted with his Lord to be continually forgiving sin, in meeting every inharmony with Truth; and this was his way of being about his Father's business. He saw and understood that in no other way could the earth be transformed and peace and harmony prevail among men and he said, 'If you forgive men their trespasses, your heavenly Father will also forgive you.'

"In order to appreciate the full value of this statement, you may ask, 'What is the Father?' The Father is Life, Love, Power, and Dominion and all of these attributes belong to the child by rightful inheritance. This is what Paul meant when he said we are joint heirs with Christ to the God Kingdom. This does not mean that one has more than another. This does not mean that the eldest son gets the larger portion and the other half is divided by measure to the remaining children. To be a joint heir, with Christ, to the Kingdom means to be an equal participant in all the blessings of the God Kingdom.

"Sometimes others accuse us of making ourselves equal with Jesus. That is because they do not understand what is meant by joint heirship. I am quite certain there is not one among us that would say he was on the same plane of enlightenment as the great Master, with his great white purity. This joint heirship means to have the possibility of the same power, the same strength, the same degree of understanding. And yet there is not one among us that does not realize the full truth of the promise of Jesus to all of God's children, to every true disciple, that they may be full participants in all the qualities of the Godhead as fully as he is. We fully recognize his meaning when he said, 'Be ye perfect even as your Father in heaven is perfect.' We know full well that that great soul never for a moment asked of his disciples a mental or moral impossibility. When he saw and asked perfection of man, he knew that he asked only that which man can live up to. A great many have taken false comfort in the belief that they never can be as perfect as the Master is perfect. They argue that he was Divine and that, because of his divinity, he did marvelous works which no other member of humanity could possibly do and that, therefore, it is absolutely useless to try. They say they are here with nothing better or more skillful or scientific with which to carve out life's destiny than mere human will power. The great Master made it clear that, while it did take some human will power to start, *the mere human will is not a great factor in the case, the great factor being divine understanding.* How many times did he say, 'You shall know the Truth and the Truth shall make you free.'

"Let us reduce this to the simple physics of the world about us. The moment men become fully acquainted with the truth of anything in the physical world about them, that moment they become free of their ignorant concept of that particular thing. The moment men became acquainted with the fact that the world was round and that it revolved around the sun, they became free from the antiquated idea of a flat earth and the rising and setting sun. The moment men become free from the belief that they are mere human beings, subject to human laws of life and death and the limitations which human beings have imposed, that moment they will see that they are free from all human limitations and may become Sons of God if they will. The moment they realize they are Divine, they are free from all limitations and possessed of the strength of divinity; and man knows that this divinity is the place where being comes most directly in contact with God. Man is beginning to see and know that this divinity is not something to be injected into each from without. He is beginning to know that it is the very life of each and every man.

"We know that the ideals we see in the lives of others take root in our lives and, in compliance with the Divine Law, bring forth after their kind. As long as we believe in the power of sin and see the effect of sin as a reality, the punishment of that sin will be vital in our own lives. But, as we give to ourselves and others truly righteous thoughts for all inharmonious ones, we are making ready the harvest of a great spiritual feast which is certain to follow the seedtime. Thus forgiveness has a two-fold mission. It frees both the erring and the loving one, for back of the application of forgiveness is a deep and radiant love, a love founded on principle, a love that desires to give for the joy of giving with no thought of reward save that of the Father's approval in the words, 'This is My beloved Son in whom I am well pleased.'

"These words are just as true for us as they are true of Jesus. Your sins, sickness, or discord are no more a part of God, or your true self, than fungi are a part of the plants to which they attach themselves. They are the false excrescences which have gathered upon your bodies as the result of wrong thinking. The thought of the disease and the disease are merely the cause and the effect. Erase, forgive the cause and the effect disappears. Erase the false belief and sickness vanishes.

"This was the only method of cure that Jesus ever resorted to. He erased the false image in the consciousness of the one to whom he ministered. He first raised the vibrations of his body by connecting his own thoughts with those of Divine Mind and holding his own thoughts steadfastly in accord with those of the perfection of the Divine Mind for man. Then the vibrations of his body became equal to the vibrations in Divine Mind. Having thus raised the vibrations of his own body by his steadfast thought of the Divine Perfection, he was able to raise the vibrations of the body of the applicant with the withered arm to the point where he could erase the image of the withered arm from his own consciousness. Then Jesus could say to him, 'Stretch forth your hand.' He stretched it forth and it became whole. Thus Jesus raised the vibrations of his own body by seeing the Divine Perfection for all and this enabled him to raise the vibrations of the one he healed until the image of imperfection was entirely erased; then perfection was instantaneous and the forgiveness was complete.

"You will soon find that, by fixing your thoughts and attention steadfastly on God and His divine perfection, you can raise the vibrations of your body so that they will blend so harmoniously with those of the divine perfection that you are absolutely one with the divine perfection and thus one with God. You are then able so to influence the vibrations of the bodies of others with whom you come in contact that they see the perfection that you see. Thus you may fulfill the divine mission and your part is complete. Or you may see imperfection and thus lower the vibrations until imperfection is the result but if you do this, you cannot escape reaping the harvest of the seed you have sown.

"God works through all to carry out His perfect plan and the perfect, loving thoughts continually going forth from the hearts of all are God's own message to His children. It is these thoughts that keep the vibrations of our bodies in direct touch with the divine and perfect vibrations; and this seed is the Word of God that finds lodgment in every receptive heart, whether man be consciously aware of his divine nature or not. We are approaching more fully to our divine inheritance when we can keep our thoughts so fully upon our divine perfection and the divine perfection of all, as held in the Mind of God, that the vibrations of our body are in direct harmonious accord and one with the divine vibrations sent out from the Mind of God. But, in order to bring forth the abundant harvest of spiritual understanding, our thoughts must continuously vibrate with, and lay hold of, the perfect harmonious thoughts from Divine Mind, or Mind of God, to man, His beloved son. We soon find we have the power to enslave or to free ourselves, as well as to forgive every sin of the whole human family through our attitude of thought, word, or deed and, through the vibrations thus released, to the whole world. Once having chosen to shape our thoughts along definite lines, we soon find that we are sustained by Omnipotence itself and find, as we go through the discipline necessary to assure ourselves of mastery, that it is a glorious privilege — this power which we have to free ourselves and our fellow-men from bondage through the process of divine thinking.

"All of Jesus' healings were on the basis of removing the mental cause. So we find that it is necessary to reduce the idealism of Jesus to practical demonstration and, by so doing, we find we are only doing that which he enjoined us to do. Many sins vanish at the first few rays of light shed into the dark concept, while others more firmly rooted in consciousness require patience and perseverance to overcome. The forgiving love of Christ must prevail if we do not obstruct but give it full sway. True forgiveness purifies and blesses all and begins in the heart of the individual. This is, at first, a thought reformation and thus, a resurrection. Realizing that God is the only Mind and this mind is pure and holy will do much to keep one holding steadfastly and worshippingly the Truth that the Mind of Christ is having its perfect way in you and establishes you in these harmonious constructive thought-currents. You become aware that you are always in the ever-flowing stream of the loving thoughts which God is pouring out to His children.

"You will soon know that you are fast approaching a period in which you will be living in a world of thinkers. You will know that thought is the most potent agency in the universe. You will soon recognize that thought is the mediator between Divine Mind and every bodily ailment or discord in the world. If you practice looking immediately to the Divine Mind, the Kingdom within, when discord or inharmony arise, you are immediately united with Divine Ideas and you will find that Divine Love is ever ready to give its healing balm of pure love to those who seek.

"Jesus lives today to wipe out of human consciousness the power and reality of sin and its effects. Fresh from the heart of Love, he came understanding the relation between God and man; and in his fearless, free recognition of Spirit as the only power, he proclaimed the supremacy of Divine Law which, when understood and applied to every act of living, will transform suffering men into radiant beings and usher in the only real kingdom of perfect citizenship, the Kingdom of Heaven upon earth." Here Jast ceased talking.

CHAPTER XII

THE sun had disappeared below the horizon and the beautiful afterglow, which foretold a peaceful night, was flaming across the entire expanse of sky. It was the first evening free from wind or storm that we had experienced in ten days and all were quietly drinking in the magnificent display of color. A quiet sunset on the Gobi can enrapture one into a reverie of forgetfulness of all things. The colors do not glow and shine; they seem to dart here and there in great beams, as though invisible hands were operating colored searchlights. At times it seemed as if these invisible hands were attempting to show the full range of the spectrum and the many variations of color to be obtained in the combinations. A wide band of white light would appear; then branching off at an oblique angle would appear a wide band of violet. From this violet a band of indigo would shoot out and along the side of the indigo a band of blue would appear and so on until the whole atmosphere seemed charged with wide bands of color. Then they would combine and blend again to the band of white, which seemed quite stationary. Again, they flashed out in fan formation, with beams of every color shooting in all directions. This gradually subsided into a solid golden color which caused the undulating sands to appear like a sea of heaving molten gold. This display continued for about ten minutes; then it faded into a haze of mottled blue, yellow, green, and grey, which seemed to drop from the heavens like a robe of night, and darkness was upon us. So quickly did the darkness surround us

114

that a number of the party expressed startled surprise at its suddenness.

The leader of the expedition turned to Bagget Irand and asked if he would give us his version of the people who had inhabited the region and established the cities like the one that lay in ruins below us. He began by saying, "We have written records that have been carefully kept from generation to generation for over seventy thousand years and these records place the date of the founding of the city, the ruins of which lie below this camp, more than two hundred and thirty thousand years in the past. The first settlers came from the west as colonists many years prior to the founding of this city. These colonists settled in the south and southwest; and as the colonies gradually developed, some of the people moved north and west until they inhabited the whole land. As fertile fields and orchards were established, the colonists laid the foundations for cities. At first these were not large but, as years went by, it was found convenient to gather in these centers for closer fellowship in art and science.

"Here temples were built; not as places of worship, for the people worshipped every moment by the life they lived. Living was always dedicated to the Great Cause of life; and while they lived cooperating with the Great Cause, life never failed them. During this time it was quite common to find men and women thousands of years old. In fact, they did not know death. They passed from one accomplishment to a higher attainment of life and its reality. They accepted life's true source and it released its boundless treasures to them in an unending stream of abundance. But I have digressed; let us go back to the temples. These were places where written records of any attainment in knowledge of the arts, science, and history could be preserved for those who wished to avail themselves of them. The temples were not used as places of worship but as places where the most profound scientific themes were discussed. The acts and the thoughts of worship in those days were carried out in the everyday life of the individual instead of being set aside for a particular group of people or at specified times.

"They found it more convenient to have broad smooth thoroughfares as means of communication; so they developed what you call paving. They found it convenient to build comfortable homes and, therefore, developed the method of hewing stone and of making brick and the mortar necessary to hold them in place, to fashion their homes and the temples. These things you have already discovered. They found that gold was a most serviceable metal, as it did not tarnish. They found means for collecting it from the sands, then from the rocks, and at last a way to manufacture it, so that it became very common. The people found the way to produce other metals as they were needed and these became plentiful. Then, instead of these communities living by agriculture alone, they began to supply those that tilled the soil with manufactured articles as conveniences for a wider range of operations. The centers grew and developed until they became cities of one to two hundred thousand people.

"Still they had no temporal heads or rulers; all governing was entrusted to advisory bodies that were selected by the people themselves. Delegations were sent to, and received from, other communities. Yet the people promulgated no laws or rules for the conduct of the individual, as each person realized his own identity and lived by a universal law governing that identity. There was no need for man-made laws; there was need only for wise counsel.

"Then an individual here and an individual there began to wander away. At first they were the more dominating souls and they would push on, while those that were inclined to plod would hold back; and unconsciously there came a separation, as the love faculty had not been fully developed by all. The separation grew wider and wider until a very dominating personality set himself up as king and temporal ruler. Since he ruled wisely, the people — with the exception of a few who felt that they could see the future of this separation — acceded to his rule without taking a thought to the future. These few withdrew into communities of their own; and from that time on they lived a more or less secluded life, always attempting to show their fellows the folly of separation. They became the first order of the priesthood; the king established the first order of temporal rulers; and from then on their devious ways may only be followed by deep study and research. There are a few that have preserved the simple teachings and have lived to follow them. But in the main, life has become very complex to the majority. In fact, so complex has it become that they refuse to believe that life is a simple form of living a well-balanced life cooperating directly with the Principle of all life. They fail to see that their way of living is the complex and hard way and that the simple life cooperating with the Principle of all life is the more abundant life. In this way they must go on until they know a better way."

Here the speaker paused, standing silent for a moment, and a picture flashed before our vision. The picture was stationary at first, as has already been described; then it became animated, the forms began to move, and the scenes changed momentarily, or at his direction, as he explained each scene. He seemed to be able to hold or reproduce the scene at

117

will, as questions were asked and answered and explanations given.

The scenes were those which were supposed to have been enacted in the ruined city below where we were camped. They did not contrast to any marked degree with scenes of a populous Oriental city of today, save that the streets were broad and well kept. The people were well clothed in raiment of good quality, their faces were bright and cheery, and there were no soldiers, paupers, or beggars in evidence. The architecture attracted our attention as the buildings were well and substantially built, and of very pleasing appearance. Although there seemed to be no attempt at display, one temple stood out magnificently beautiful. We were told this temple was built entirely by volunteer hands and was one of the oldest and most beautiful in the land. On the whole, if these pictures were representative, the people must have been contented and happy. We were told that soldiers did not make their appearance until after the second king of the first dynasty had reigned for nearly two hundred years. That king, in order to keep up his retinue, began taxing the people, and soldiers were appointed to collect the taxes. In about fifty years, poverty began to show in isolated places. It seems that about this time a portion of the people who were dissatisfied with the kingdom and with those who had assumed the rule, withdrew. Bagget Irand and his people claim the lineal heritage of this race.

As the night was well advanced, Bagget suggested that we adjourn and retire, since it would be much pleasanter to make an early morning start. About three hours of the full noonday heat was uncomfortable for travel and the time of winter storms was fast approaching.

CHAPTER XIII

WE WERE up early the next morning and at break of day were on our way to Bagget Irand's home village, which we reached on the evening of the twelfth day. We were welcomed by the party which had visited us the last afternoon of our stay on the desert and were invited to stop for a few days' rest. We were shown to quarters that were a real luxury after those we had experienced on the desert. After we had made ourselves presentable, we stepped into the next room and found a number of friends. They greeted us heartily and we were told the village was ours and that every door was flung wide to receive us.

The Governor of the village, through an interpreter, welcomed us, telling us we were to dine at his house, and were to start immediately. We filed out of the room, led by the Governor with a guard of two soldiers, one on each side, as was the custom of the country. Next came the leader with our hostess and our Chief with the beautiful lady. Then came Emil and his mother. I walked with them, the rest of the party following.

We had proceeded but a short distance when a poorly dressed child stepped from the crowd which had assembled and asked in the native tongue if she might speak to Emil's mother. The Governor brushed her aside unceremoniously, saying that we could not be bothered with such as she. Emil's mother grasped our arms and the three of us stepped out of the ranks to hear what the girl had to say. As we did this, our hostess hesitated and as she stepped out of the ranks the whole company stopped. Emil's mother spoke to

119

the Governor, saying she would like to have the rest go on and get seating arrangements completed and that by that time we surely would be there.

Meanwhile, she was holding the girl's hands in hers. As the company moved on, she knelt down and, putting her arms around the little girl, said, "Dear one, what can I do for you?" She found that the child's brother had fallen that afternoon and they thought his back was broken. The child begged the lady to go with her to see if she could not help him as he was in great pain. Emil's mother arose, explained the situation to us and told us to go on, that she would go with the child, then come in later. The leader said that if it was permissible, he would like to go along. Emil's mother invited us all to go; so we turned aside and followed her and the girl as they walked hand-in-hand, the girl fairly leaping with joy. Our hostess told us that the girl was certain her brother would be healed by the great lady. As we neared the house, the girl bounded ahead to tell her family we were coming.

When we came up to the door, we saw that the house was but a mud hut of the lowest order. Emil's mother must have interpreted our thoughts, for she said, "Although it is a hovel, warm hearts beat within." At that moment the door was thrown open, a gruff masculine voice spoke, and we stepped inside. If the hut looked wretched from without, it was doubly so from within. It was scarcely large enough for us to crowd into and the ceiling was so low that we could not stand erect. A dim witch light burned and cast a weird light upon the hard faces of the father and mother as they sat amidst their squalor.

In the far corner, on a mass of musty straw and vile-smelling rags, lay a lad not more than five years old, his face drawn and ashen pale. The girl knelt beside him, holding his face in both of her hands, one pressed against each cheek. She was telling him that he was going to be perfectly well again, as the beautiful lady was already there. She removed her hands, moved aside to give him a clearer view, and for the first time she saw the rest of the party. Instantly her expression changed and a great fear seemed to pervade her whole form. She dropped her face in her folded arms and her form shook with a convulsive sob as she cried out, "Oh, I thought you were coming alone." Emil's mother dropped on her knees beside her, put both arms around her and held her close for a moment. She became silent and Emil's mother said she would send us away, if the girl wished to have us go. The girl said she was only surprised and frightened; that we need not mind her, as she was only thinking of her brother.

Then Emil's mother said, "You love your brother dearly, do you not?" The girl, who could not have been more than nine years old said, "Yes, but I love everyone." The conversation was interpreted to us by Emil, as none of our party spoke the language. Emil's mother said, "If you love your brother so much, you can help to heal him," and she told the girl to take the position she had been in and to place her hands on each side of his face. Then Emil's mother moved so that she could place her hand on his forehead. Almost instantly the moans ceased, the boy's face lighted up, his little form relaxed, a perfect calm settled over the whole scene, and the child slept quietly and naturally.

Emil's mother and the girl sat as they were for a few moments; then, with her left hand the lady gently removed the girl's hands from the boy's face, saying, "How beautiful he is, how strong and fine." Then Emil's mother removed her hand ever so gently and, as I happened to be standing near her, when she extended her left hand I reached out my hand in

121

order to assist her to her feet. As her hand touched mine such a thrill went through my whole body that it left me perfectly helpless. She sprang lightly to her feet and said, "For a moment I forgot myself. I should not have taken your hand as I did, for momentarily I seemed to be overwhelmed, so great was the power that was flowing through me." I recovered my composure almost instantly. The others did not notice as they were all deeply engrossed in what was going on around them.

The girl had suddenly thrown herself at Emil's mother's feet and, clasping each in one of her hands, was frantically kissing the coverings. Emil's mother reached down and with one hand turned the fervent tear-stained face upward, then knelt and clasped the child to her and kissed her eyes and lips. The child put both arms around the mother's neck and both were motionless for a moment; then that strange light began to pervade the room and it grew brighter and brighter until every object seemed to be suffused with the light and nothing cast a shadow. The room seemed to be expanding. The father and the mother of the two children had sat on the dirt floor in stony-faced silence thus far. They arose and the expression on their faces changed to blank dismay, then to fright, and the man bolted through the door, nearly upsetting the leader of the expedition in his haste to get away.

The mother of the household threw herself prostrate at the side of Emil's mother and sobs shook her frame. Emil's mother placed her hand on the woman's forehead, speaking in a low voice to her. Presently the sobs ceased, she drew herself to a half-sitting, half-kneeling position, and saw the transformation that had taken place in the room. The expression on her face changed to one of terror; she rose hastily to her feet and started to run from the room. Emil reached out his hand, and took one of her hands while the beautiful lady took the other. They held her hands thus for a moment and the frightened expression changed to a smile.

We looked around and, in place of the hovel we had entered, we were in a moderately comfortably furnished room with seats, table, and a clean bed. Emil walked over and picked up the boy, still sound asleep, from the heap of musty straw and rags, placed him tenderly on the clean bed and drew the covers over him. As he did so he stooped and kissed the child's forehead as tenderly as any woman could have done.

Emil's mother and the girl arose and walked to where the mother of the household stood. We all gathered around them. The mother sank to her knees and, grasping the feet of Emil's mother, began kissing them and entreating her not to leave. Emil stepped forward and, stooping down, took the woman's hands and drew her to her feet, all the time speaking quietly to her in her own language. As she stood erect, the old soiled garments she had been wearing were changed to new ones. She stood in mystified silence for a moment, then threw herself into the outstretched arms of Emil's mother. They stood in this attitude for a moment, when Emil reached out and, placing his hands upon their arms, separated them.

Then the girl rushed forward with outstretched hands crying, "See, see, my things are new." She turned to Emil's mother who stooped and picked her up. The child put her arms around her neck with her face close to her shoulder. The leader of the expedition was standing just back of Emil's mother, and the child reached out her hands over the mother's shoulder toward him, lifted her face, and gave him a happy smile. The leader stepped forward and held out his hands. The child clasped them, saying that she loved us all but not as much as she did this dear lady, meaning Emil's mother.

Emil said he would go and find the father. He returned in a few moments, bringing the frightened and half-sullen father with him. Still, we could see that underneath the sullenness there was a deep appreciation. We prepared to leave and as we left, the mother of the household asked if we would not come again and was told that we would see her again the next day.

We hurried away to the Governor's house, fearful lest we had kept the party waiting. Although the time had seemed hours, we could not have been away more than thirty minutes. I am certain it all happened in much less time than it has taken me to write about it. We arrived at the house just as the rest of the party were taking their seats at the table. The leader of the expedition asked if he might sit by our Chief and it was so arranged. It was easily seen that he was very much agitated and the Chief said afterwards that the man was so moved by what he had seen that he could scarcely keep quiet. The seating arrangements were: the Governor at the head of the table, at his right Emil's mother, then Emil, the beautiful lady, our Chief, and the leader of the expedition. On the Governor's left sat our hostess, then Emil's son and his sister. I mention these arrangements because of what happened later.

After we all were seated, the meal progressed very nicely until it was about half concluded. The Governor addressed Bagget Irand, asking him if he would not continue a talk he had started a short time before, which had been interrupted by the arrival of a governor from a larger village. Bagget Irand arose and said they had been talking of the similarity of the lives of Buddha and Jesus. With our permission he would continue the talk but it would be necessary to speak in a language that the host understood, as it was not customary to have an interpreter unless the speaker did not speak the language of the people. Jast volunteered to act as interpreter but, when the Governor understood the situation, he insisted that Bagget Irand should speak in English and Jast would interpret to him, as the greater majority spoke and understood English.

Then Bagget Irand went on to say: "We can compare in our own thoughts what the power of man would be if all the attributes of true Spirit dominated his every action, deed, and thought; or, as Jesus said, 'When the Holy Spirit has come upon you.' In this he referred to the time when the God Power should fully determine the lives of all His children. This means God manifest in the flesh. In reality, do we not see this spiritual unfoldment for all people coming through the lives and teachings of the seers and prophets in a greater or lesser degree, in proportion as their spiritual unfoldment approaches the perfect development of God manifesting throughout all his children?

"It is quite evident that those who have followed steadfastly the true ideals of life which they have perceived as coming directly from God—and thus connecting God with man—have made the greatest attainments toward nobility of character, purity of soul, and moral grandeur of life. Should those who seek to follow them by incorporating their ideals in individuality be able to accomplish as they have accomplished, the world must finally accept that the lessons they gave out, as their lives, presage the undeveloped possibilities of all God's children.

"Still none of these has claimed that they have

reached the ultimate perfection which God has chosen for His children; for Jesus said, "He that believes in me, the works that I do shall he do also, yet I go unto the Father.' Both Jesus and Buddha said, 'You shall be perfect even as your Father in heaven is perfect.'

"These sons of God are not mythical persons but their lives and work have spoken definitely in the lives and hearts of men all down through the historical ages. There have been myth and tradition woven about their lives. The effective test is for one who is interested in their lives and characters personally to accept and apply their teaching in his everyday life. The fact that the ideals expressed by these great men are those held as the ideals that govern all truly great people is a further proof of their truth. If one attempts to refute the lives of these great men, one may as well ask why great religions exist. It is most certain that they are the foundation and bear the footprints of an irresistible instinctive urge, or instinct, which has presaged the great depth and true basis of the betterment of mankind; and they outlive and outshine any other possible attempt to relieve the human family from limitation and bondage.

"The records of these men's lives are preserved for us and their lives become a legitimate source of inquiry and research if we will but open our hearts, pursue this inquiry with an open mind, and make their lives, teaching, and ideals our very own. In no other way can we enter in and become one with their lives. This has been the inspired message of every true seer since the world's history began. Two, at least, of these spiritually enlightened men, Jesus and Buddha, brought to fruition the great possibilities they taught. They have said, in almost the same words, 'I am the way, the truth, and the light of life

126

for all men.' In the divinity of their attitude they assumed they could truly say, 'I am the light of the world. He who follows me, who walks and lives as I have lived, shall not walk in darkness but shall have Eternal Life and shall be abundantly free from all limitations.' Both, in nearly the same words, said, 'To this end was I born and for this cause came I into the world, that I should bear witness unto the Truth. Everyone that is of this Truth, hears my voice.' These words must have had a direct bearing upon the true unfoldment of the Christ life in every child of God.

"Do not all the religions of the world reveal a higher power in man that is struggling to be free from the limitations of sense? The scriptures of the different races are outward expressions of this intelligence. The Book of Job in your Bible antedates all your history. It was written in this country and its mystical meaning has been preserved through all the changes that have taken place, although it has been nearly smothered by the addition of folklore. Though the people were nearly all consumed, the mystical word of Job will never be consumed, for he that dwells in the secret place of the Most High dwells in the shadow of the Almighty One. Another thing we must see is that *all scriptures came from religion and not religion from the scriptures.* The scriptures are a product of religion, not the cause of it. The history of religion came out of experiences, while the gospels came out of all religions.

"You will soon find that unity of purpose and effort will be the most potent means to attain any desired end. Instead of numerous people thinking in all directions and pulling in as many, they will think as one. Then man will know what it means to give a long pull and a strong pull and a pull all together. Then you will see that when the unity of will is set in

127

motion all things are possible. When man casts the selfish satanic thoughts from his consciousness, the battle of Gog and Magog will cease; and this will not be accomplished by any outside deity.

"When Jesus said, 'My words are spirit and they are life,' he touched that inner word that created all things; and he knew that his word was filled with a life essence and the moving power that would produce the thing he desired. If these words would ring through the souls of all men and nations, they would know that they have access to the fountain of Eternal Life which flows from God.

"Some may express the Christ by seeing the Christ enthroned just back of the heart, the seat of love. From this throne see the Christ directing every activity of your body in perfect accord with God's immutable law and know that you are cooperating with Christ in the ideals received direct from the Divine Mind. Then see the Christ seated on His throne, expanding and including every atom, cell, fibre, muscle, and organ of your whole body. In fact, He has expanded until your whole body is the pure Christ, the only begotten Son of God; the pure temple where God is at home and loves to dwell. From this throne you can call upon every center of your whole body. You can say to those centers that you are positive, loving, powerful, wise, fearless, a free spirit. You are pure with the purity of Spirit. No mortal thought or desire or impurity can come near you. You are immersed in the pure Christ. The Spirit of life in the Christ makes you the pure temple of God. Here you may pause and say, 'Father, in this as well as in all things, reveal the Christ, Your perfect Son to me.' Then bless the Christ.

"When you have realized the Christ, you may hold out your hand and, if it is gold you want, the gold will be there." Here he held out his hands and there was a circular disc of gold somewhat larger than an English sovereign in each hand. He passed them to those sitting at his right and left and they, in turn, passed them on until the discs had made the rounds of the whole table. (We preserved them and had them examined by experts, who pronounced them pure gold.)

"If you wish to assist others, see the Christ enthroned in them as he is in you and speak to the Christ in them as though you were talking directly to them.

"If you want to get a clearer view of any subject than you have at present, let the Christ speak mentally to the abstract soul of that subject or thing. Then ask the intelligence within the thing to tell you about itself.

"God's children are just as necessary to Him in the carrying out of His perfect plan as any plant, flower, or tree is; and it is necessary for them to cooperate in the perfect way which He sees. It was the withdrawal of man from this perfect plan to cooperation that threw the world out of balance and caused great waves to sweep over and destroy the greater portion of His children. It is the perfect thought of Love cooperating with Poise and Power in the hearts of God's children that holds the earth in balance. When they dissipated that force in thoughts of sin and lust, it swung so far out of balance that the great waves rushed over and nearly annihilated man and the work he had accomplished. At that time man had accomplished far more than he has today. But God cannot control man's thoughts of love and balance, or hate and unbalance; they are for man to control. When the thought force that threw the earth out of balance was dissipated by the great cataclysm it had brought on, then God in His mighty power could restore the earth to its proper equilibrium or balance; but as long as man's thought held sway, God was powerless to act." Here Bagget Irand ceased speaking and took his seat.

We had noticed that our host, the Governor, had betrayed signs of uneasiness and considerable excitement; and when Bagget Irand took his seat, our host's excitement burst forth in an exclamation which carried the meaning of "Dog, dog of a Christian, you have defamed the name of our fair Buddha and you shall suffer!" At this he pulled a cord that hung from the ceiling near him. Instantly, three doors flew open at the opposite end of the room from where he was sitting and in rushed thirty soldiers with drawn swords. He had risen from his seat at the table and the two guards who had accompanied him and were standing just back of his chair during the meal stepped forward to his side. Raising his hand, he gave an order. Ten of the soldiers came forward and arranged themselves along the wall back of where Bagget was sitting; two stepped forward and took their stand just back of and on each side of his chair. The commander walked forward and stood at attention a short distance from where the Governor and his two guards stood. Not a word had been spoken by any of the company and scarcely a move had been made. We sat completely overcome by the suddenness of the change.

Then a deep silence seemed to fall and a strong light blazed forth in the room at the head of the table just in front of where the Governor stood. Every eye was upon his face as he stood with upraised hand, as though about to give another order, but his face was ashen pale and a look of horror had come over it. A dim form seemed to be standing on the table before him. All heard the word, "Stop," pronounced clearly and very forcefully and the word itself stood out in flaming letters between the dim form and the Governor. The Governor seemed to understand, for he stood as though transfixed and as rigid as a statue. By this time the dim form had taken definite shape and we recognized it as that of Jesus as we had seen him before. But the thing that amazed us was that another dim form was standing beside him and it was this form that was holding the attention of the Governor and all the soldiers. They seemed to recognize and to fear the dim form that stood by the side of Jesus far more than they did Jesus. As we looked around they were standing perfectly rigid. As the second form grew more distinct, it raised its right hand as Jesus had done and at this every sword fell from the soldiers' hands, clattering to the floor. The room re-echoed with the sound, so deep was the stillness. The light seemed to glow with a far greater intensity; indeed, so intense did the light become that we could scarcely see.

The commander was the first to recover. He stretched forth his hands, exclaiming, "Buddha, our Buddha, the Sublime One." Then the Governor exclaimed, "It is indeed the Sublime One," and threw himself prostrate on the floor. The two guards stepped forward and assisted him to his feet, then stood silent and immovable as statues.

A shout went up from the soldiers, who had arranged themselves at the far end of the room. They rushed pell-mell along each side of the table and crowded together at the head, shouting, "The Sublime One has come to destroy the dogs of Christians and their leader." At this Buddha stepped back upon the table until he could look them all in the face and raised his hand with the words, "It is not once that I say 'Stop!' not twice that I say, 'Stop!' but three times that I say, 'Stop!'" Each time when he pronounced the word it appeared in flaming letters as it had when Jesus had pronounced it; and the words did not disappear — they remained.

The crowd of soldiers again stood and stared as though transfixed, some with their hands in the air, some with one foot from the floor, in the attitude in which they happened to be at the instant Buddha had raised his hand. He again walked to where Jesus stood and, placing his left hand under Jesus' raised arm, said, "In this as in all things I support the upraised hand of my dear brother here." Then he placed his right hand upon Jesus' shoulder and they stood in this attitude for a moment; then both stepped lightly from the table, while Governor, commander, guards, and soldiers fell back, staring at them with blank, ashen faces. The Governor sank into his chair that had been moved back until it was against the wall of the room and every one of the company gave vent to a sigh of relief. I think scarcely one of us had drawn a full breath during the few minutes it took to enact this scene.

Then Buddha locked his arm in that of Jesus and the two walked directly in front of the Governor. In words that were thrown from him with such force that they seemed to rebound from the walls, Buddha said, "Dare you for one moment call these, our dear brothers, Christian dogs? You, who but a short time since, ruthlessly cast aside a little child who was pleading for help for a loved one. This dear, great soul here turned aside and heeded the call." Here he dropped Jesus' arm, turned, and with hand extended toward Emil's mother, stepped toward her. As he continued, he turned half-way around so that he could look from the Governor to Emil's mother. It was plainly seen that he was deeply stirred. He fairly flung the words from him as, looking at the Governor, he continued, "You, who should have been the first to respond to the call of that dear child, shirked your duty; and then you call the one that did respond, a Christian dog. Go and see the restored child, whose body but a moment before was torn and writhing in anguish. See the comfortable home that has been reared from the hovel that your acts are partially responsible for thrusting upon these dear ones. See the miserable heap of filth and rags that this dear soul," turning to Emil, "raised that child's body from. See how tenderly he raised him and placed him in a clean, neat couch. Then see how, after he had raised the little body, the filth and rags disappeared. And you, licentious bigot that you are, were sitting at ease in the purple that is to be worn only by those that are pure. You dare to call these that have in no way harmed you or another, Christian dogs; and you call yourself the follower of Buddha, the High Priest of the temple here. Shame! Shame! Shame!"

It seemed that every word would hit the Governor, the chair, and the draperies about him and rebound. At any rate, they were sent with such force that the Governor trembled and the draperies fluttered as though they were blown by a strong wind. There was no question of an interpreter; the Governor did not need one. He understood perfectly, although the words were spoken in the purest English.

Buddha turned and walked to the two men who had received the gold pieces and asked if he might have them. They handed the discs to him and, with these in his open hand, he walked back to the Governor and addressed himself directly to him, saying, "Put forth your hands." The Governor did so but they were trembling so greatly that he could scarcely hold them out. Buddha dropped a disc in each hand and almost instantly it disappeared. Buddha said, "See, even pure gold will fly from your hands"; and the two discs landed almost simultaneously on the table before the two men that had first received them.

Buddha reached out both hands, placed them on the Governor's outstretched hands and, in a mild, calm voice said, "Brother, you need not fear. I do not judge you. You are only judging yourself." He held his hands thus and stood quietly until the Governor became calm. Then he removed his hands and said, "You are quick to fly with your swords, to redress what you judge to be a wrong. But remember, when you are judging and condemning other men you are judging and condemning yourself."

He returned to Jesus' side as he said, "We who know, stand together for the common good and brotherly love of all mankind." He again linked his arm with Jesus' and said, "Well, Brother, I think I took this affair out of your hands entirely. It is all in your hands now." Jesus replied, "You have done nobly and I cannot thank you enough." They turned and bowed, then arm in arm walked through the door and disappeared.

The room at once broke into a hubbub of voices. The Governor, commander, soldiers, and guards all crowded around to shake our hands. Everybody was trying to make himself understood at the same time. The Governor spoke to Emil and he raised his hand for silence. As soon as he could be heard, he said the Governor would like us again to be seated at the table.

When all had resumed their seats and quiet had been restored, we saw that the commander had drawn the soldiers back into formation at each side of the table and back of the Governor's chair which had been drawn near the table. The Governor arose and, with Emil acting as interpreter, said, "I allowed my zeal to get the better of me, for which I am heartily ashamed and doubly sorry. I do not think it is necessary for me to say this after what has happened. I believe you can see by my attitude that I have changed and I wish to ask Brother Bagget to arise and accept my most humble apology. Now will the whole company arise?" After they had risen, he said, "I ask you all to kindly accept my most humble apology. I extend to you all a most hearty welcome and, if you so desire, I hope you will stay among us always. If you wish a military escort at any time, which I judge you do not, I shall—and I know the commander here will also—deem it a high honor to be of service to you. I cannot say more. I bid you all good night. Before you go, I wish to say that everything I have is at your command. I salute you and the soldiers salute you also; and they will escort you to your quarters. Again I bid you good night and salaam to you in the name of the Great Buddha, the Celestial One."

The commander, making profuse apologies and saying that he was certain we were in league with the Celestial One, with five of his soldiers escorted us to our quarters. As they left they gave us a salute, which is executed by forming a half circle around the commanding officer and presenting their swords so that their points just touch the point of their commander's sword. Then they turned quickly, swept off their hats, and salaamed very low, touching one knee to the ground. This salute is given only on great state occasions. We accepted the salute as best we knew how and they departed. We went into the house, immediately took leave of our friends and host, and prepared to go to our tent. There were so many of us that the rest house had not accommodated all; so our camp had been set up in the enclosure at the rear of the house.

As we reached our camp, the leader sat down on a camp cot and said, "Although I am dead tired, there is absolutely no use in my going to bed before I know something more; and I am going to serve notice that I intend to sit here all night unless I am somewhat enlightened. I can tell you this thing has gone much farther than skin-deep with me tonight. You fellows sit around and say nothing and appear as wise as owls." We told him he knew as much as we for we had never before witnessed anything like what had taken place.

Someone suggested that it had been staged for our special benefit. The leader fairly jumped at him. "Staged! Why man, the crowd that could stage anything like that would be worth a million a week of anyone's money. And the Governor—if he was acting, you can choke me, for that old fellow was thoroughly frightened. I am going to admit that I, for a few moments, was just about as frightened as he was. Away back somewhere there is a dim suggestion that that old fellow had a red-hot reception staged for all of us. That outburst was not just for Bagget Irand. When those soldiers came rushing forward, there was too much of a triumphant note in their voices. If I am not mistaken, they were all in on a deeper play than we were aware of. That same something suggests that, for a moment, they thought Buddha had come to help them. When they saw the whole scheme had gone against them, their very bodies dropped and, when I think of it, I remember that they dropped their swords. Say, did not Buddha have power? Just see how he threw those words at the old Governor. He seemed much more powerful than Jesus did; but then it was his side that needed bolstering up, for our side, under the circumstances, had all the best of that event.

"But didn't the old Governor get a boost? I'll bet by this time he feels like lifting himself over a fence by his own boot straps. When Buddha clasped his hands, it actually looked to me as though the fellow jumped right out of his old self. We are going to hear a lot more of him before another sun, if I am not mistaken, and I am going to predict that it is good, for that old one is a power in this land. If he got the wonderful uplift that I did out of it, I would not mind being in his boots after all."

We talked of the things we had seen and heard and, before we realized how the time was passing, dawn began to break. The leader arose, stretched his arms above his head, and said, "Who needs any sleep? I don't believe I do, after listening to you talk." We lay down, fully dressed, for an hour's rest before breakfast.

CHAPTER XIV

WHEN we were summoned to breakfast that morning, the leader was the first one up. He hurried through his morning toilet like an eager schoolboy. After he had finished, he urged everybody to more haste. We finally went in to breakfast and found Emil and Jast. The leader went over and sat between them and asked questions throughout the meal. The moment we finished eating he arose from the table and wanted to rush off again to see the house that had grown in fifteen minutes, as he expressed it. He put his hands on Jast's shoulders and said that if he had two like Emil and his mother what fun he would have going around and growing houses for poor people. The he said, "But would I not make the landlords in New York look sick? I pay rent to those fellows." Then Emil said, "Suppose they would not let you grow houses for them?" "Well," he said, "I would do it anyway and, after I had grown them and they would not use them, I would pick them up bodily and put them in and chain them." All of us laughed heartily over these things.

We had always taken the leader for a quiet, reserved man. He told us afterwards that the things he had seen set him on his feet, so that he could not help asking questions. He also said this had been by far the most interesting expedition of his whole life, although he was familiar with the world's most remote places. He definitely decided to assist us to organize a second expedition to carry on the excavation work under the guidance of our friends. But this was prevented by his sudden passing.

We could scarcely restrain him from going directly to the new house. We finally compromised with him and Jast and one of the others walked with him to where he could see it. They returned from this trip in about thirty minutes and he was jubilant. He had seen the little house and it was real. He said that it brought back ever so vividly a boyhood vision that he had. Then he told of seeing himself going around with fairies, building houses for poor people and making them happy.

As our party was so large, it was thought best not to go in a body to see the little house. It was arranged that we were to go in groups of five or six. The personnel of the first group was to be Emil, the leader, one or two of the ladies, and myself. We started out and Emil's mother and our hostess joined us. We walked on until we came in sight of the house. The little girl came running out to meet us and threw herself in Emil's mother's arms, saying that her brother was strong and fine. As we reached the house, the mother of the child came out, dropped to her knees in front of Emil's mother and began telling how she adored her. Emil's mother put out her hands and assisted her to her feet, telling her that she must not kneel to her; that what she had done for her she would do for anyone; that she was not to praise her, but the Great One, for the blessing she had received. The little boy opened the door and the mother motioned us to go in. We followed the ladies in, with our hostess interpreting for us. There was no question that the house was there; it contained four rooms and was very comfortable. It was surrounded on three sides by the most miserable hovels. We were told that the occupants of the hovels were going to move away, as they thought the house was of the evil one and might destroy them if they stayed.

We heard more from the Governor also. At about

eleven that morning he sent the commander and a detail of soldiers to invite us to lunch with him at two that afternoon. We accepted and, at the appointed hour, there was a guard waiting to escort us to the Governor's house. The reader will understand there were no fine equipages in that country; so we used the only mode of locomotion we had—walking.

When we arrived at the Governor's house we found that a number of Lamas, including the High Priest, from the nearby monastery had preceded us. We learned that this monastery housed from fifteen to eighteen hundred Lamas and was of considerable importance. The Governor was one of the higher body of priesthood of the monastery.

We at first expected a lively discussion but soon learned that the luncheon was only for the purpose of getting acquainted with the members of our party. Our friends were very well acquainted with the High Priest, as they had met a great many times and had worked together. This, it seems, the Governor did not know until that morning, as the High Priest had been away from the monastery for about three years and had returned only the evening before our arrival.

During the course of the lunch, we found that these Lamas were well educated, had a broad out-look on life, had traveled a great deal, and two of them had spent a year in England and America. They had been told by the Governor of what had occurred the evening before and, in all, a very close friendly feeling was evidenced before the luncheon was concluded. As for the Governor, we found him a very congenial fellow and the only mention made of the previous evening was to the effect that a great enlightenment had come to him. He plainly said that until the last evening he had harbored a great hatred for all foreigners. We were obliged to carry on all conversation through interpreters, which is not very satisfactory when one wishes to get at the deep thoughts of the other.

Before we left, we were extended a cordial invitation to visit the monastery and spend the next day there as their guests. At Emil's suggestion we accepted and the next day spent with them was very pleasant and instructive. We found the head Lama a very remarkable man. The friendship that began that day between him and our Chief afterwards ripened into a close and life-long brotherly understanding and he was of untold service to us in the later research work which has been carried on in the adjoining country.

CHAPTER XV

EMIL TOLD us that there would be a meeting that evening somewhat like the one we had attended at his home village the year before and invited us all to attend. We accepted with keen delight.

Just before the appointed time for the meeting, Emil, his mother, and I went to the child's house for the mother and sister, as they had asked to go with us. On the way from the house to the meeting place, we passed a number of dilapidated mud huts. The little girl stopped before the door of one of these, saying that a blind woman lived there and asked Emil if she might go in and bring her to the meeting if she wished to come. This he gave her permission to do. The girl opened the door and stepped into the hut, while we stood waiting outside. In a few moments she reappeared in the doorway and said the woman was afraid and motioned for Emil to come to her. He went to the door and they conversed for a few moments. Then both entered the place.

Emil's mother said, "That child will yet be a power for good among these people for she has the ability and determination to carry out whatever she undertakes. We have decided to let her handle this in her own way, except that we direct and assist her, guided by what we perceive as the thing best suited to give her more confidence in herself. Let us see the method she takes to induce this woman to be present at the meeting. The fear that these dear ones hold toward us is beyond belief. Many are moving away from the vicinity of the little one's home, when you would think they would besiege us to assist them in obtaining homes like it. This is the reason we are obliged to be so careful of their feelings. While we desire to lift them all from their surroundings, as we did those dear ones, they flee from us at the first sign of our approach."

I asked how she was able to help the child and her parents as she had.

She answered, "That was through the attitude of the child and through her we could help them all. She is the balance wheel in that household and through her we will reach this dear soul and many more here," indicating the huts that were about. "It is these that we love to bring close to our hearts. That little home was not brought forth in vain."

Here Emil and the girl appeared, saying that the woman wished the girl to wait for her and they would come on in a short time. We went on, leaving the girl with the blind woman.

When we arrived at the meeting place, nearly everyone had assembled and we found that the High Priest of the monastery was to be the head spokesman of the evening. We were told that Emil had met this Lama about eighteen months before and a warm friendship had been formed at that time. This meeting had been arranged and we were there at the Lama's special request. This had been the occasion for their visit to us the last day on the desert. We were also told that the Governor was next in authority under this man. A number of the surmises of our leader were confirmed but our friends showed no fear whatever.

Emil said that both of these men were going to be their close friends from that time on and that it was seldom they were able to reach those as high in authority as these two, but they were content to let matters move on slowly. We were told that the preceding evening was the third time that Jesus and

Buddha had appeared visibly to help them and they seemed pleased that we had been there to witness the scene. They did not seem to look upon it as an added triumph but as an opportunity to enable them to cooperate and work with these people.

At this time the girl entered, leading the blind woman. She found a seat for her charge, a little to the rear and at one side of the room. After the woman was seated, the girl stood facing her, holding both of her hands and, in a moment, she stooped forward as though she were speaking to the woman in a low voice. Then she straightened up and, letting go of the woman's hands, placed her little hands over the woman's eyes and held them there for two or three moments. This movement seemed to attract the attention of everyone in the room, from the High Priest down. All arose and stood looking at the child and the woman, while the High Priest walked rapidly over and placed his hand upon the child's head. As he did this the child's frame shook visibly but she did not change her position. The three remained thus for a few moments, then the child removed her hands and cried out joyously, "Why, you are not blind at all, you can see." She pressed her lips to the woman's forehead, then turned and walked over to our Chief.

She seemed somewhat bewildered and said, "I spoke in your language. How did I do that?" Then she said, "Why does not the woman see she is not blind any more? She can see."

We looked again at the woman; she had risen and, clasping the robe of the High Priest in both her hands, she said in the native tongue, "I can see you." Then she looked around the room with a half-dazed air, saying, "I can see you all." She let go of the Priest's robe and burying her face in her hands, sank back into the seat she had been occupying, sobbing,

"I can see, I can see, but you are all so clean and I am so dirty. Let me go away."

Then Emil's mother stepped forward. Standing directly back of where the woman was sitting, she placed both her hands on the woman's shoulders. The Priest raised his hands but not a word was spoken. Almost instantly, the woman's garments changed to clean new ones. Emil's mother removed her hands from the woman's shoulders. The woman arose and in a dazed, perplexed way looked around. The Priest asked what she was looking for and she replied that she was looking for her old clothing. Then the Priest said, "Do not look for your old clothes. See, you are clad in clean new garments." She stood for another moment as though wrapped in perplexed thought; then her face lighted up with a smile, she bowed very low and resumed her seat.

We were told that this woman had been blind for more than twenty-five years and that the blindness had been caused when the eyeballs were pierced by fine shot from a gun in the hands of one of a band of robbers.

The excitement had been so great that our party had crowded around. The leader, meanwhile, had worked his way to the little girl, and they were conversing in low tones. He told us afterwards that the child spoke English very well. Our hostess had interpreted when the conversation was carried on in the native tongue.

Someone suggested that we should be seated at the table. As we began taking our places, the woman arose and told Emil's mother, who had stood quietly at her side, that she would like to go. The child stepped forward, saying she would go with her and see that she arrived home safely. Here, the High Priest asked the woman where she lived and, upon being told, said she must not go back to that filthy place.

The girl said she was expecting to have the woman stay at her house and, arm in arm, they left the room.

When we were all seated, the dishes were placed on the table as though by unseen hands. At this, we saw the Priest start and look around in wonderment. But when the edibles began to arrive in the same way, he turned to Emil's mother, who was seated at his right hand, and asked if this was a regular occurrence with them, saying that he had never been privileged to witness this before. He turned to Emil, who was interpreting for us, as though he would like some explanation. Then Emil explained they were able to use the same power that was used to heal the blind woman, to bring forth all that they needed. It was quite plain that he was still puzzled but he said no more until the meal was well under way.

He arose and, with Jast acting as interpreter, said, "I believe I can see more deeply than I imagined human beings could be privileged to see. Although my whole life has been spent in the Order of the Priesthood, in which, as I supposed, I was serving my fellow men, I observe now that I was but serving self far more than I was serving my brother. How this brotherhood has been extended tonight — and my vision has followed that extension! I am just now allowed to see what a narrow life we are living; that we have lived despising everyone but our own people. This vision allows me to see that you are of the sublime as well as we and what a celestial joy that vision allows me to behold."

Here he paused with his hands half upraised, while a look of surprise and pleasure flooded his countenance. He stood in this position for a moment, then he said, "This is nonsense. I can and will speak in the language you speak. Why can I not do this? I see

146

what your thoughts were when you told me that
there was no limit to man's ability to express. I find
that I can speak directly to you so that you may
understand."

He paused for a moment as though to pick up the
thread of thought, then spoke without the aid of an
interpreter. We were told afterwards that this was
the first time he had spoken in English. He continued, "How beautiful it is to be able to speak directly
to you in your own language. With the broader
vision this has given me, I am consumed with wonder
as to why men look upon any of their brothers as
enemies. It comes so clearly that we all must be of
the same family, the same source, the same cause.
Would that not determine that there was room for
all? If one brother chooses to see differently than we
do, why should we say that he must perish? I see we
cannot interfere for, if we interfere, we but retard
our own development and isolate ourselves. If we do
this our house will fall and crumble about our own
heads. Now I see, instead of a limited race, a universal, eternal, limitless All — All coming from the One
and returning to the One.

"I see that your Jesus and our Buddha lived by the
same light. Their lives, as well as all others who live
in and by that same light, must merge into the One.
I am beginning to see where it all converges. The
crystal clear light is shedding its radiance over me. I
believe that man elevates himself to a regal position
but often, when he has gained that position, he can
no more see his brother as regal. He wishes to be
regal himself and his brother to be the serf.

"Why did that child place her hands on the eyes of
that dear one whose eyes were closed? I see now that
it was because that child saw more deeply than I,
who should have had more knowledge. It is what you

call a mighty love. It is the same which caused Jesus and Buddha to stand together; at which I did wonder but I wonder no longer. Now I see that it does no harm to include you all for, as we include you, we have the good that you have and that can but benefit us. I can see that the power which will always protect you will protect me. The armor that protects me will in the same way protect you. If it protects you and me, it must protect all. The dividing line has disappeared. What a celestial truth! I see your thought when you say the world is God's world and the near and far places are His. If we see the near and far places together, they will be the same to us. We live in a place surrounded by our own world, not seeing the fact that outside our little world the whole wide world surrounds us; and that world will help us if we will let it. Then to think that God surrounds one and all!

"I now see the Holy Brother's thought when he said the doors are to be thrown wide to those who are ready to receive. It is said that man shall not only give ear but he shall become that which he claims to be and, sinking self, he shall be immersed in the Brotherhood of Man. It is deeds, not fine words, that endure. I can see that the way of progress is not only barred by the creeds of others but by those of ourselves. Each is directly claiming the graces of the Most High; each attempting to build up his own by dismantling and tearing down all others. Instead of using energy to tear down, that energy should go to consolidate the whole. The most High not only made one nation of one life but of one life all the nations of the earth. The time is now come when we must choose between creeds and the Brotherhood of Man. Creeds are but the conjurings of man. The faith that moves mountains still slumbers in the seed of the plan. The height and grandeur are still there for

148

man to attain. The law of enlightenment has preceded that of miracle. This law of enlightenment is the higher law of Love and Love is the Universal Brotherhood.

"I now see that all that is needed is for each to return to the fountain of his own religion, to remove all false interpretations and cast out all selfishness. In each will be found the pure gold of the alchemist, the Wisdom of the Most High; your God and my God, not many gods of many people, just one God. It is the same God who spoke to Moses from out of the burning bush; the same God of whom Jesus spoke when he said that through prayer he could summon legions to sustain him in his hour of mortal struggle in doing the work the Father had given him to do; the same God to whom Peter prayed when he was released from prison. I now see the mighty power that can be summoned to the aid of those who will cooperate in the Brotherhood of a consecrated life."

Here he raised a glass and held it for a moment in the palm of his hand. He became very still and the glass crumbled to dust. Then he continued, "The armies before Jericho knew of this power when they blew their trumpets and the walls of the city fell. Paul and Silas knew of it when they released themselves from prison."

Again he stood for a moment in perfect silence. The building rocked and swayed, great tongues of lightning flashed, and two great masses of rock became detached from the mountainside about a mile away and came rumbling down into the valley below. The villagers came running from their houses in terror and we could scarcely restrain ourselves from doing the same, so violently did the building rock and sway.

Then he lifted his hand, all became quiet, and he continued: "Of what avail are armies or navies, when man knows that God has this power and that His true sons may use it? You can sweep an army away as a child blows the down from a thistle. As for great battleships, they may be dissolved like this glass." Here he lifted the plate upon which he had deposited the powder that now represented the glass. He breathed upon it lightly; it burst into flames and disappeared entirely.

He again resumed, "These legions come not to do your work or my work or to use man as their instrument; man may call upon them to encourage, sustain, and comfort him in his work as master of every condition of life. With this power man may still the waves, control the winds, quench the fire, or direct the multitude. One may use them only as he has mastered them. He may use them for the good of the whole human race or he may use them to drive home the meaning of man cooperating with God. One who is able in his divinity to call upon these legions, knows beyond question that he can use this combined power only in true service to humanity, for he knows that it will consume him as well as defend him."

Here the speaker paused for a moment, stretched forth his hands, and in a measured, reverent voice, said, "Father, it is our great pleasure to have these, our dear friends, with us tonight. It is with a true and humble heart that we say 'Thy will be done.' We bless them and in blessing them we bless the whole world."

He sat down as calmly as though nothing out of the ordinary had taken place and all our friends were calm; but the members of our party were on tiptoe with excitement. Then the invisible choir broke forth with "All know the power that's in a name, and man may proclaim himself the King and then with humble mien, that man may rule himself supreme."

During this remarkable demonstration of power we had been unconscious of our tense, nervous condition but, as the choir finished, we became conscious of this and we had seemed to need the music to help us relax. When the last strains of music had died away, we arose from the table and gathered around our friends and the Priest.

This gave the leader and our Chief opportunity to ask questions; and the Priest, seeing their interest, invited them to spend the night at the monastery with him. They bade us good night and left the room together.

We were scheduled to leave at noon next day. It was arranged that only Jast and Chander Sen should accompany us to our outfitting point, where Emil would join us and the three would return with us to the village of our winter quarters. After these arrangements were completed we returned to camp but did not retire until nearly daybreak, so interested were we in talking of what we had witnessed.

CHAPTER XVI

A T TWELVE o'clock, with all final arrangements complete, the expedition moved out of the village amid the cheers and good wishes of the greater number of the villagers, who had gathered to bid us goodby.

Our next stopping place, where we were obliged to cross a wide stream, was reached about six that evening. It was thought best to camp in order to prepare for the crossing, as this would consume the greater part of the next day. Since there was no bridge or boat, the crossing was accomplished by sliding across on a large cable made of plaited leather thongs that had been stretched across the river. The individual members of the party experienced no difficulty in negotiating the cable. The chief difficulty was in getting the horses and mules across. This was finally accomplished by making a strong sling from leather straps and arranging it so that an attachment would fit over and slide along the leather cable. This sling was first securely fastened around the animal's body, then secured over the cable, and the animal was pushed over the bluff, where it hung suspended above the roaring torrent until it was pulled to the other bank. To this sling were attached two ropes of sufficent length to reach across the river, one serving to pull the animal across, while the other served to pull the sling back again for another animal. In this way all crossed safely.

We experienced no further difficulty and, aside from the crossing, we found the trail much better than the one we had followed going out. We arrived safely at our outfitting point, where the expedition was disbanded; and arrangements were completed for those who were to return home to go on to the seaport by the regular caravan route.

The next morning Emil joined us and, after bidding our associates goodby, we started out on our return trip to the village of our former winter quarters. We again stopped two days to rest at the bandit camp, where the two men remained, thus reducing our party to seven. These two men told their comrades of the remarkable trip they had made and the wonders they had seen. Our party was shown every courtesy, though, of course, our three friends came in for the greater honors. The leader of the band assured them that the bandits would hold the location of the cities absolutely sacred out of their respect for the consideration that had been shown them. We were told there was very little danger of this band's ever attempting to go so far away; the desert bandits never invaded the mountains nor did the mountain bandits invade the desert, for they were continuously at war with each other. So far as we know they have faithfully kept their promise.

The morning we left this camp, the leader of the band came and gave our Chief a small silver coin about the size and weight of an English shilling, with a curiously wrought inscription upon it, saying that if any of the bandit bands in that country molested us, we would gain our instant release by showing this. He told us that it had been in the possession of his family for many generations and that he cherished it very highly but he wished our Chief to have it as a token of his esteem. After examining it carefully, Emil said it was a very faithful reproduction of a coin that had been in use in the Northern Gobi many thousands of years ago. The date showed that this particular coin had been made more than seven hundred years before. He then told us that these coins were worn as a kind of charm by some of the natives of the region; and the older the coins were, the more efficacious they were supposed to be. No doubt this particular one had been prized very highly by the leader and the whole band.

From this village we continued our journey and arrived at our winter quarters in due time without further incident. We were welcomed heartily by the party which visited us in the desert and which we had left at the village where we met the High Priest.

We were again invited to share the home of our former hostess, which invitation we gladly accepted. This time there were but four of us, as seven of our associates had returned to India and Mongolia to carry on further research work. This arrangement had been suggested and agreed to in order to give us more time for the translation of the records. All was quiet in the little village and we gave every moment of our time to the arrangement and form of the symbols and characters which made up the alphabet, placing them in the order that enabled us to use them, thus giving us an insight into the meaning of the words. In this we were assisted by Chander Sen. While he was not with us all the time, he or our hostess was always at hand to help us over the difficult places. This continued until the last days of December, when we noticed that a number of people were again congregating for the yearly gathering. They were nearly all people we had met at the gathering the year before. We found that this year they were to meet in the temple and use the center room of the five upper rooms that were arranged along the ledge as already described.

We went up to this room, early New Year's Eve, in order to meet and talk with those who had gathered. We found that they were from numerous places and they told us of things that had happened in the outside world, with which we were beginning to feel we had lost all contact. Yet we had been happy in our work, the time had passed rapidly, and we were very content.

While we were talking, one of the guests came in and said that the moon was very beautiful. A number of those in the room, including all of our party, walked out upon the ledge. It was indeed a beautiful sight from that elevation. The moon had just risen and seemed to be floating through a great bank of delicate colors which were reflected on the vast expanse of snow that covered mountain and valley and the colors were continuously changing. Someone said, "Oh, the carillon will ring tonight." In a few moments the bells did begin. At first it was as though a bell located a long way off had been struck three times; then smaller and smaller ones sounded, coming nearer until they seemed but tiny bells located directly at our feet. So real was the impression that we looked down expecting to see the bells. This melody continued until it seemed as though thousands of bells were being struck in perfect harmony. The bank of color would rise until it appeared to be even with the ledge where we were standing and it would seem as though we could step out upon it, so completely did it shut out the earth below. As the color raised in undulating swells, the sound of the bells would increase until the melody filled every niche.

It appeared as though we were standing on the stage of a great amphitheatre with thousands of dim forms and faces of those listening to the bells. Then a full, strong tenor voice began to sing "America," and in an instant thousands of voices took up the words while the bells carried the melody. Thus the song

155

went booming on until the end, when voices back of us said, "America, we greet you." Then others said, "We greet the whole world."

We turned and there stood Jesus, the High Priest, and Emil. We had become so enraptured by the phenomenon that was taking place about us that we had become wholly unconscious that there were others near us. All stepped aside to let the three enter the room. As Jesus turned, we could see that remarkable light that always shone out when he was present and, as he stepped through the door, the whole room became a blaze of white light. All went in and were seated at the tables.

Jesus was seated at the first table and the Priest at our table, with Emil and our Chief on either side. This time there were but two long tables down the length of the room. There were no coverings but, as we were seated, the tables were covered with white linen and the service came on almost as quickly. The food seemed to come with the plates, with the exception of the bread. A loaf appeared on the table before Jesus. He picked it up and began breaking it, placing the pieces on a plate. When the plate was filled, a dim childish form lifted it and stood silent until seven plates had been filled and seven forms stood holding them. As Jesus broke the bread and filled the plates, the loaf did not diminish.

As the last plate was filled, Jesus arose and with outstretched hands said, "This bread which I present to you represents God's pure Life. Partake of that pure Life which is always of God." Then, as the bread was handed around, he went on to say, "When I said, 'I am lifted up,' and that by being so lifted up I would draw all men to me, I knew that, in the light of that experience, some day all would see eye to eye and know full well when they could be lifted up as I am lifted. I saw heaven right here on earth among

156

men. This is the Truth that I perceived and the Truth will make all free. Then they will find that there is but one fold and one shepherd; and if one strays, it is safe to leave all the ninety and nine, to seek the one that he may return. God may be all in all to all His children; and all are His—they are far nearer and dearer to Him than the sparrows or the lilies of the field. If He rejoices in the lilies' growth and notes the sparrow's fall, how much more does He note the growth of His dear children. Neither does He judge them more than He does the lilies or the sparrow, but holds them dear to His great cause and not one can be left out when His perfection is established.

"I could see that, if this ideal could be graven in letters of purest gold on the walls of the temples of the world's great thought, it would lift men's thoughts above the murk and mire by setting their feet on a rock, a sure foundation; where the winds and tides could lash and roar but, while men stood steadfast and true, they would be secure. Because of this security, peace, and calm they would aim to the heights where they see their true dominion. They may soar above but they will not find heaven above. They will find it right among men, and it is not reached by merely plodding on and on, in toil and sorrow and great tribulation, and then eventually finding the great Jewel. It is much more quickly reached by throwing off all materiality and the laws that thereby bind men to the eternal wheel. Then step forth, you pick up the Jewel, incorporate it, let the light shine forth, and you have gained by one direct step that which you may put off through all eternity, if you will. You will find that the soul which insists upon immediate and complete spiritual illumination and emancipation here and now and knows that his relation to God is the relation of parent and child, quickly sees that this not only makes clear the divine possibilities but that he has them to use and they will work for him as he wills. To that one, the New Testament story will not be fiction nor a vague dream that may happen after death but an ideal that is lifted up before the world, of a perfect realization of a life of love and service. That ideal is the divine accomplishment of all, here and now.

"Then will they know the vision I saw when I said, 'Many shall seek to enter in and shall not, for strait is the gate and narrow is the way that leads to eternal life.' For, without the true appreciation of the Christ Ideal and of the divine and perfect plan of the cooperation of man and God right here on this earth, the realization of this ideal is impossible and it becomes only a dream, a myth — nothing.

"The door giving access to this omnipotent and transforming alchemy of the Spirit in man is open to all at all times and the key to its opening is in the thoughts of all. When two ideals and methods of salvation or of securing the saving grace of God's love, are different, it is man's thoughts and not God that made them so. Those who close the door to the immediate blessings of God for all His children, isolate themselves from the immediate blessings that God bestows upon the Christ Child and from the spiritual illumination of the transcendent alchemy of Spirit and the all-potent powers which are theirs to use as the Christ would and should use them. When men recognize this, the leper will be made whole instantly, the withered arm will be restored, and all diseases of body and mind will vanish at their touch. Through the concentration of the spoken word, they will multiply the loaves and fishes; and as they break the bread or pour the oil for the multitude, it will never diminish but there will always be an abundance left. They will calm the raging sea or tempest by their command and gravitation will be overruled by levitation, for their command is the command of God. Then will they know my thoughts when I gave forth my opening message to the world as I left the temple that day, when I said, 'the time is fulfilled and the Kingdom of God is at hand,' and, 'have faith in God and nothing is impossible to you.' All who believe they can do the works that I do and will come forth and do them may do even greater works than I have done. They will know that it is a process of living the life, believing and knowing; then absolutely nothing is impossible to them.

"They will know that the Holy Spirit, the whole of the Divine Spirit in them, says today just as it did long ago that, if they hear its voice and harden not their hearts, they will find they are the light of the world and they that follow that light shall not walk in darkness. They will know that they are the door by which all enter into the light of life and those who will go in and out by that door will find eternal peace and great joy and will discover that now is the accepted time.

"They will find that the Christ but opens the door to their own souls and the spirit that dwells therein is the all-potent alchemy as limitless as the universe of God is limitless. The alchemy will dissolve and transmute all manner of sickness; will erase clean the mortal life of guilt and the effects of sin; will illuminate the soul with the perfect light of Wisdom; will emancipate from and dissolve the darkened conditions of human life into the perfect light of life. Thus, they will see they are not only children of nature but children of God as well. They will bring forth the absolute perfection of the individual and thus will perfect the race. They will bring forth the ideal and the divinely inspired prophecy concerning

159

the final destiny of man here on earth, the identity of Father and Son, which is the second birth, the perfect mastery of man over every condition and circumstance."

Here Jesus paused and the lights became brighter and brighter. Then pictures began to appear. The scenes were glorious bursts of splendor. The pictures would come on, a transforming hand would reach out and touch them, and they would develop into a great whole and become beautiful.

There came on a great war scene. We saw men struggling and fighting against each other. The cannons were belching forth flames and smoke. Shells burst overhead and among the great throng and men were falling on every hand. We could hear the roar and din of battle. Indeed, it was so real that it seemed certain a battle was in progress but, as the transforming hand reached out and over it, all became calm in an instant. As those who had been fighting so furiously but a moment before looked up, the hand traced in flaming letters that seemed to spread over the whole scene: "Peace, Peace, the Blessed Peace of God surrounds you. You can only hurt and destroy the mortal. But one of God's own you can not destroy and you are all His own children. You can neither hurt nor destroy each other."

Then, for a moment, it seemed that men were again determined that the struggle should proceed; this determination showed on many faces, especially those of the leaders. But it appeared that the more determined they became to go on, the less cause there seemed to be for a display of force. It also seemed that the more they attempted to discharge the weapons of destruction, the less effect they had; for try as they would, not a weapon could be used.

Then the hand went on to trace, "Behind every

160

cloud of storm or war, if men will only look, they will find God. They will find that God did not create the clouds of storm or war, that man created them and, if they will look beyond and see, they will always find God's hand upraised in peace. War is not sent or ordained by God; when men war with each other they are entirely outside of God's province or power. They are entirely immersed in a man-made realm where God cannot interfere in any way and they will be obliged to go on in this way until they see the fallacy of such strife. If one is sufficiently strong in his realization of God-power, knows his ability to co-operate with that power, and does cooperate, he can stop a war instantly, just as you saw it stopped in this picture."

Then Jesus continued, "I chose the way of the cross. It was not my Father's choice for me but my choice, that all might see they can so perfect the life and body that although it be destroyed it can be rebuilt and become more triumphant."

The lights grew even brighter, until every vestige of limitation had disappeared; not a wall surrounded us, not a roof overhead, not a floor beneath. We all stood together in boundless space. The twelve disciples came and arranged themselves near the Great Master but did not surround him, for his presence stood out far more prominently than any other, with a never-to-be-forgotten brilliance and purity. The invisible choir boomed out, "His Kingdom is here, for, of, and among men. Now henceforth and forever, one man, one God." The transforming hand again appeared and traced the words, "His Kingdom is here now, among men, henceforth, forever, one man, one God." Then directly over Jesus' head were traced the words, "ALL FOR ONE, ONE FOR ALL."

161

Buddha then appeared, standing at Jesus' right. The Priest and Emil walked to them and knelt before them, Emil at Buddha's right and the Priest at Jesus' left. Jesus clasped Buddha's partly upraised hand. They raised their free hands until these were over and just above the heads of the two who were kneeling and said, "Peace! Peace! Peace! A glorious peace rests over all. We receive you, our dear brothers, into the great council of God's beneficent Love; and that Love and Fellowship includes the whole world." Then all those assembled bowed their heads and made way as the four passed through the assembly. As they passed, the disciples and a number of those assembled followed and all passed on until they disappeared from our vision.

When they had begun moving through the assembly, the invisible choir had chanted, "We make way for these mighty brothers of Love; for that Love, the mighty Love of God, redeems and unites all mankind in the great council of God's Love, the Brotherhood of Man and God." As they passed from view, the great bell boomed out twelve strokes. Then, for a moment, the bells pealed a merry refrain and thousands of voices joined in: "We bring the glad New Year and a brighter day for all the world."

Our second year with these great souls had closed.